Bibliographic software and the electronic library

edited by Terry Hanson

University of Hertfordshire Press

First published 1995 in
Great Britain by
University of Hertfordshire Press
Library and Media Services
University of Hertfordshire
College Lane Hatfield
Hertfordshire AL10 9AB

© University of Hertfordshire Press

ISBN 0-900458-51-8

Designed by
Beverley Stirling

Cover design
by Colin Boyter

Page layout by
Kate Douglas

Typeset at
University of London Computer Centre

Printed by Watkiss Studios Limited

Contents

Introduction
Part 1   The nature of bibliographic software

Chapter 1   What is bibliographic software?
page 8   *Terry Hanson, University of Connecticut*

Chapter 2   Importing downloaded records into bibliographic software
Page 21   *Terry Hanson, University of Connecticut*

Part 2   Case Studies

Chapter 3   Standardising on *Pro-Cite* at the University of Portsmouth
Page 29   *Terry Hanson, formerly University of Portsmouth*

Chapter 4   Library support for *Reference Manager* at a
page 41   School of Medicine
                John Cox, Wellcome Centre for Medical Science

Chapter 5   *EndNote* on the Apple at the Imperial Cancer Research Fund
Page 56   *Jane Milligan, Imperial Cancer Research Fund*

Chapter 6   *Papyrus* at the University of Manchester and the
Page 63   CHEST licence
                Sarah Davnall, Computer Centre, University of Manchester

Chapter 7 A trial of PC bibliographic database and formatting packages
Page 70   *E. R. Carter, Thornton Research Centre, Shell Research Ltd.*

Part 3 Copyright

Chapter 8 Electrocopying from databases
Page 84   *David Slee, Centre for Legal Studies,*
University of Hertfordshire

Chapter 9 Staying within the law
Page 95   *Professor Charles Oppenheim, Department of Information Science, University of Strathclyde*

Appendices

Appendix 1 Contact addresses for leading bibliographic
Page 108 software packages

Appendix 2 BIDS and bibliographic software
Page 113

Appendix 3 Internet discussion lists for bibliographic software
Page 115

Appendix 4 List of criteria for evaluation of bibliographic software
Page 117

Appendix 5 User trial questionnaire
Page 120

Page 124 **Bibliography**

Notes on contributors

Introduction

Software for the management of personal collections of bibliographic references has been available since about 1983, although today's products are, of course, in most cases, vast improvements over those early versions. For most of this period the popularity of what has become known generically as bibliographic software has increased only slowly and gradually among the intended user community of academic researchers.

In the last two or three years, however, its popularity has begun to grow more rapidly as its importance to the effective use of the emerging electronic library has been recognised. In particular the following factors have led to the increased interest.

■ The greater availability of PCs among academic researchers. In most universities and research organisations the PC is now rightly recognised as an essential productivity tool without which most researchers would find it very difficult to function

■ The increased availability of end-user oriented bibliographic databases principally on CD-ROM. The latter has revolutionised access to bibliographic information in favour of 'end-users'. Downloading references from these sources and importing them into the personal database is a logical next step.

- The improved friendliness and functionality of the software itself and in particular the greater ease with which records from end-user databases can be imported.
- The increased awareness among librarians, as information intermediaries, of the importance of bibliographic software and their consequent efforts to spread the word among their research colleagues.

The main focus of this book is on this latter point. It aims to introduce the reader to bibliographic software from the perspective of the librarian or information intermediary working in a library which is making increasing use of bibliographic and full text databases. In three sections the papers discuss the software, its applications and the nature of the librarian's role and copyright issues.

Part 1 has two papers describing bibliographic software and its principal features. The first is concerned with locating bibliographic software within a database software spectrum ranging from general purpose database management packages such as *dBase4* to highly specialised text retrieval packages, such as *Pro-Cite* and *Reference Manager*, and the second examines the issues and problems relating to importing records downloaded from external sources such as online and CD-ROM databases.

Part 2 comprises five case studies looking at the use of particular packages in a variety of organisations: two universities, a medical school and two very different research establishments.

Part 3 has two, complementary, accounts of the thorny question of copyright in relation to downloading from electronic databases and the extent to which librarians and users may be constrained in their information provision activities.

Finally, there is a selected, but extensive, bibliography of recent writings on bibliographic software and a product guide. The suppliers have agreed to provide readers with demonstration versions of the software on disk (mention this publication when ordering).

It is hoped that the book will be of interest to librarians and information professionals in all types of organisations, that they may find it helpful in selecting suitable software for their particular cirumstances, deciding what their role should be in this area and how they should exercise it.

Chapter 1 What is bibliographic software?
Terry Hanson, Head of Research and Information Services, University of Connecticut

There are many different types of database and many different types of database software. In this book we are concerned only with software designed for use with microcomputers, although, of course, much of what is written will apply equally well to larger machines. Typical applications of database software might include the management of personnel records, company products, customer records, library borrowers or bibliographic references. Not so typical applications include long textual documents such as entire articles, books or committee minutes.

It is difficult to offer a universally acceptable definition of a database but for our purposes here we are principally concerned with the need to store collections of information in such a way that it is possible to retrieve specific information flexibly and quickly. The operative word here is 'collections' because databases normally deal with large collections of records with a common data structure. The record type can vary from a relatively short and highly structured record such as a name and address file to a long and relatively unstructured record such as the full text of a law case or newspaper article. Either way the information is stored as a collection of separate records.

Database software can be categorised as follows:

Programmable/Relational DBMS software
The most famous database software packages are general purpose database management system (DBMS) products used for a wide variety of applications. Examples include the legendary *dBase* in all its incarnations, *FoxPro, Paradox*, etc. In addition to allowing for simple database creation and keyboard data entry, this type of software is programmable, whereby the user can, by learning a proprietary programming language, develop specific, highly customised database applications, such as an inter-library loans system in a library, a video bookings system or an inventory control system. This is the real strength of this software and it is thus seen, perhaps primarily, as an application generation tool. In this respect it is not intended for the uninitiated.

This software is also likely to be relational. This means that separate databases can interact, or cross refer, when necessary. For example, a company might wish to maintain databases containing information about products (specifications etc.) and their suppliers (names and addresses etc.). One way to do this would be to make a record for each product and add the supplier information to each record as necessary. This would involve a lot of repetition where, for example, one supplier supplied many different products. The relational approach would involve making two databases one for the suppliers and one for the products. The products database would have an automatic link to the suppliers database so that the required details could be retrieved when required.

Databases created using software in this category tend to be highly structured with fixed field lengths and predictable content, such as telephone numbers, addresses, prices, product codes, dates, etc. Access to information is achieved through 'query' languages or routines. A query would be capable of conducting a complex search, sorting the retrieved records and presenting them in a customised format. An emerging standard in the area is the so called Structured Query Language (SQL) and many packages now boast this capability.

Flatfile
A flatfile database package would lack the programming language and relational features of the above category. Databases created would be independent as would the individual records and fields within. As a consequence they are considerably easier to use and do not require the user to master an esoteric programming language. Typical applications would be name and address lists, book references, inventories, etc. The user would design the record structure and data entry screen and then type in the data. Fixed length fields are again the norm. Queries would be relatively straightforward using standard textual and numeric operators. Examples of flatfile packages include *File Express, Rapidfile, Q&A, PC File*, etc.

Clearly both categories of software discussed so far could handle bibliographic records, to a point. Where they would have some difficulty though is in the variable field lengths required in text-based records. It is for this reason principally that both these categories are unsuitable for text-based applications such as bibliographic databases. But to make this point is not to criticise *dBase* etc. DBMS software was simply not designed for text applications. For this reason 'text retrieval' software has emerged.

Text retrieval software (1-6)
Text retrieval software tends to be much less structured than the software discussed above. As the name implies it is designed to handle records containing, primarily natural language text, such as is contained in bibliographic references and abstracts. Where this is the case the field lengths need to be flexible in order to accommodate variable length titles, etc. In other words, the user of the system does not determine the parameters of the field content except in very general terms. For example, it is the author of an article that determines the number of characters required in the title field and not the creator of the database.

As with flatfile packages databases are created without the need to be familiar with programming routines. Each database is independent from the others and within a record each field is independent of the others. There are no fields, for example, which have their content determined automatically by a mathematical relationship between certain other fields.

Access to textual databases is normally through natural language keywords collected together into index (inverted) files. Searching procedures normally adopt the standard Boolean model whereby keywords are combined using the 'operators' AND, to narrow down a search, OR to broaden out a search, and NOT to exclude keywords from the search.

Text retrieval software can be sub-divided into two general categories: packages which are intended for relatively short and relatively structured records, such as bibliographic references and those which are designed to handle long 'full text' documents such as entire articles, law reports, committee minutes, etc. There is much overlap in the sense that packages in both categories can perform tolerably well in the other area.

Full text
As the capacity of storage devices become ever greater so the temptation grows to use them for the full text of documents of all kinds. CD-ROM in particular is proving to be very popular for this purpose and there are now many products providing full text of journal articles, books, poetry, newspapers, press cuttings, law reports, etc. When long textual records such as these are stored there is an obvious need for information retrieval facilities to allow access to any part of the document(s). Two very good and well known packages in this area are *AskSam* and *Personal Librarian*. The former achieved some notoriety by being used to index the Iran-Contra hearings in the US Congress. The latter is used in such products as the *Financial Times* on CD-ROM.

With this software each word, apart from designated stop words, is indexed so as to allow fast and flexible retrieval. On the question of information retrieval from full text documents an important debate is in progress between those who believe that the individual user has a unique requirement and should be allowed by the search software to define each search using whatever keywords they want ('free text' searching). Opponents would maintain that even full text databases, especially those that comprise many different documents, like journal and newspaper articles or books, benefit greatly by offering structured searching using controlled subject indexing for each record. The essence of the argument for free text searching is that in long textual documents (whether full text or records with long, well-written abstracts) the text itself will contain sufficient indication of the subjects under discussion for good quality retrieval software, using techniques such as relevance ranking, to be able to identify all records on a given topic. Good text retrieval software packages should offer the ability to use both approaches.

Non full text
Finally, we arrive at our destination – well almost. We are concerned with software designed for managing short, text-based, records such as bibliographic references. We have a final distinction to make, between those packages, such as *Inmagic*, *Cardbox* or *Headfast* which will happily accommodate this type of record, and the likes of *Pro-Cite* and *Reference Manager*. The former packages are marketed as general purpose text retrieval software but are customisable, to an extent, by the user. As an indication of their adaptability *Inmagic* sells companion products which provide 'pre-defined' customisation for use in libraries *(Library Guide)* and law firms *(Legal Guide)*. There are many published articles and reports illustrating how these packages have been used for special projects (6-14). An example of the adaptability of *Headfast* is its use as an interface in CD-ROM databases such as the European Community bibliographic database SCAD from Context Ltd/ EPMS and *BookFind-CD* from Book Data.
    Pro-Cite and *Reference Manager* are examples of what might be called specialised text retrieval or bibliographic software, or even personal bibliographic software. They are designed for a very specific purpose which is to help academic researchers to manage their personal collections of

Chapter 1

bibliographic references and it is this category of software upon which we shall now concentrate.

Bibliographic software
What distinguishes software in this category from others is the extent of specialisation. In the same way that database management software is available for other precise applications such as estate agencies or for dental practices so personal bibliographic software aims to satisfy those whose stock in trade is bibliographic references, i.e. academic researchers. All the packages referred to in each of the categories above would be perfectly capable of handling bibliographic references but it is personal bibliographic software that will do so most effectively, with the least fuss and make the fewest demands on the user's time and computer expertise.

The number of packages that fall into this specialised category is growing all the time and it is very difficult for potential new users to gain an overall knowledge of the market and so make confident purchase decisions. Although this paper is not meant as a buyer's guide some general observations of the market may prove helpful.

The market may be divided between the expensive and the inexpensive and generally, although certainly not always, price and quality are closely associated. At the relatively expensive end are the overall market leaders *Pro-Cite* and *Reference Manager* and *EndNote Plus* along with *STN Personal File System* (a host specific package for STN only). Of these packages *Reference Manager* is the most specialised. It is designed specifically for biomedical scientists. At the inexpensive end are the likes of *Papyrus* and *Paperbase*.

Currently, the only one of these packages available in a Windows version is *Reference Manager* (launched in May 1993). *Pro-Cite* and *EndNote Plus* should have made this migration by the middle of 1995. Although *Papyrus* does not have a *Windows* version it does run under *Windows* and can use the *Windows* clipboard (see page 69 for details). The *ideaList* package from Blackwell is already available for *Windows* but by dropping its pre-defined input, importing and output formats it ceases to be a bibliographic software package. *Pro-Cite, Reference Manager* and *EndNote* are all available in both IBM and Macintosh versions. *Pro-Cite, Reference Manager* and *Papyrus* are networkable with record and file locking, and *Pro-Cite* has read-only status available within the network and single user versions.

This list is far from being exhaustive but the products noted include the market leaders and are, all easily available in the UK, although mostly produced in the US. The main exception to the price/quality relationship is *Papyrus* which represents remarkably good value for money although it lacks some of the polish and ease of use of *Pro-Cite, Reference Manager* and *EndNote Plus. Papyrus*, in fact, is available for an even better price for UK universities through a site licence arrangement negotiated by CHEST (Combined Higher Education Software Team). The details of the CHEST site licence are set out in Chapter 6.

Details of prices, compatibility and availability of the packages referred to in the text are provided in the Appendix. Further comments on the four leading packages *(Pro-Cite, Reference Manager, EndNote Plus* and *Papyrus)* are given alongside the description of the main features below.

Standard features of bibliographic software

Although the range of packages is growing constantly they have certain basic features in common.

Ease of use
This is perhaps the most important feature given that the intended market is academic researchers who, in the main, will not be computer experts. The very fact that these packages are so specialised makes the task of building in friendliness and ease of use simpler since assumptions can be made about the types of information that will be handled as indicated below.

It is very difficult to characterise accurately the relative friendliness and ease of use of the main packages. What appeals to one user may be disliked by another. All four leading packages have their adherents on the friendliness front and it would be unwise to attempt to make any comparison or judgement here.

Pre-defined data structures
With general purpose database software the user must first create a data structure by naming the fields and designing the data input screen into which records will be typed at the keyboard. Because personal bibliographic software can assume that the records will be bibliographic in nature then it can offer pre-defined data structures or input formats. Typically, therefore, these packages offer several formats for standard bibliographic documents such as books, journal articles, book chapters, theses, audio visual materials, etc. The user simply selects the appropriate form for each item to be added to the database. Needless to say, a single database may contain any combination of available data structures.

Among our four packages *Pro-Cite* offers twenty data structures, *Reference Manager* has thirty three in the recently released Version 6, *EndNote Plus* has fourteen (seventeen for the Mac version) and *Papyrus* has eight. *Pro-Cite* and *EndNote* also allow the user to create additional data structures.

Pre-defined output formats
Assumptions can also be made about how selected records can be printed. With the general purpose packages the user would have to use the built-in report generator to determine the appearance of printed records. With our bibliographic software packages they all offer a range of pre-defined output formats based on standard bibliographic styles adopted by organisations such as the American National Standards Institute (ANSI) or the American Psychological Association (APA), or by individual journals as instructions to authors.

The number of pre-defined output styles varies constantly and it is, therefore, difficult to give accurate figures on the actual number supplied with each package. *Pro-Cite* offers about thirty output formats as standard, *Reference Manager* offers only three but provides nearly 200 optional extra *Common Journal Formats* and *Papyrus* offers more than 120. *EndNote Plus* has about 240 for the Mac but only twelve in the DOS version (but this will change with the release of *EndNote Plus* for *Windows* in 1995). All the packages provide the means to create additional formats as required.

Automatic generation of bibliography from manuscript
A very popular feature among active researchers is the ability to compile a reference list for appending to a written paper by scanning the paper and recognising the embedded references. If the latter are in a suitable format, such as (Bloggs 1992), then the software will match up the reference in the text to the details in the designated database and compile the list. The packages vary in terms of file formats that can be recognised. They also vary in terms of the form in which the embedded references can be recognised, whether as record numbers from the database or as (author, year).

Pro-Cite, Reference Manager and *EndNote Plus* in their Macintosh versions all recognise at least Microsoft *Word* and *Macwrite II*. In the versions for DOS *Pro-Cite* and *Reference Manager* support Microsoft *Word* and *WordPerfect*. *EndNote Plus* also supports these plus *Word* and *WordPerfect for Windows*. *Papyrus* supports *Word, WordPerfect* and *Wordstar* in both DOS and Windows versions.

Boolean searching
The standard model for searching text databases is the Boolean approach whereby keywords are combined using the operators AND, OR and NOT. This technique is used on most, if not all, bibliographic databases online, on CD-ROM or diskette. Bibliographic software packages also use this approach, although, as with online and CD-ROM databases, the actual interface presented to the user will be different with each package. With the release of *EndNote Plus* all the packages now support the Boolean search method and since the release of version 2.0 of *Pro-Cite* there is not much difference between the packages in terms of search speed. All are very fast even on large files.

Chapter 1

Batch importing of records
In some ways this is the most important feature of all. With the features already described many potential users may be convinced of the usefulness of this software. However, at some stage they will begin to wonder about the length of time it takes to type in records at the keyboard and conclude that far from being a labour-saving device it would require the services of a full time typist to enter all the records needed. The ability to import batches of records downloaded from, for example, CD-ROM databases in the user's academic library, is thus a very important and attractive facility.

The different approaches to importing and their associated problems will be examined in the next chapter.

Other features
In addition to these principal features most packages will also be capable of a range of other tasks:
- Flexible sorting of selected records down to several levels.
- Output to either printer or a disk file for further manipulation in another package. Most packages rely on an external word processor for page and character formatting but *Pro-Cite* offers basic formatting as well as the option to use a word processor. The word processors supported are generally the same as those for the generation of bibliographies from a manuscript file.
- Duplicate detection. This is rarely a completely accurate process. The final decision on whether a record is a duplicate must be made by the user. However, the packages are getting better in this area and both *Pro-Cite* and *Reference Manager* now allow the user to vary the detection arrangements to produce more accurate results.
- Search and replace and global addition of text. These are extremely useful features for all kinds of purposes. *Pro-Cite* is particularly strong in this department and *Reference Manager* now has a global keyword addition feature.
- Merging of databases.
- Producing structured bibliographies. This is another very useful *Pro-Cite* feature which can produce bibliographies listed by, for example, keywords taken from the Descriptor

field. *Papyrus* can also produce a keyword headed listing but *Pro-Cite* can generate the heading from any field.
■ Authority lists. Many packages provide access to the index files as 'look-up', or 'authority' lists when searching or editing. *Pro-Cite* is an exception in that the index file cannot be viewed but authority lists can be created.

References

1   ELECTRONIC DOCUMENTS, 1 (3), 1992. Issue devoted to text retrieval software.

2   GILLMAN, P. *Text retrieval*. Taylor Graham, 1992.

3   SIEVERTS, E.G. and HOFSTEDE, M. Software for information storage and retrieval tested, evaluated and compared. Part 1: general introduction. *Electronic Library* 9 (3), 1991, 145-154. See also bibliography.

4   SIEVERTS, E.G. et al. Software for information storage and retrieval tested, evaluated and compared. Part 2: classical retrieval systems. *Electronic Library* 9 (6), 1991, 301-318. See also bibliography.

5   *VINE*, 88, September 1992. Issue devoted to text retrieval software.

6   COALE, K. Advances in text retrieval. *Macworld* 10 (12), 1993, 168-172.

7   BUKTOVICH, N.J., BROWNING, M.M. and TAYLOR, K.L. The Reference Expert: a computerized database utilizing *Inmagic* and a worm drive. *Database* 14 (6), 1991, 35-38.

8   DAVIES, J. *Cardbox-Plus* and the design of the Anglo-Welsh Database Source. *Program* 22 (1), 1988, 84-88.

9   DAVIES, J. Fangwel. A program to generate complex author bibliographies from a *Cardbox-Plus* database. *Program* 23 (2), 1989, 189-196.

10 HO, P. Making the most of *Inmagic* software. *Database* 14 (5), 1991, 86-87.

11 JOHNSON, J.M. Info – A *Cardbox-Plus* index to sources of computer and telecommunications information. *Program* 22 (2), 1988, 177-181.

12 MENK, B. Using *Inmagic* to create a database for historical photographs. *Database* 11 (5), 1988, 111-114.

13 STOVER, M. and GRASSIAN, E. Toward an automated reference information system: *Inmagic* and the UCLA Ready-Reference Information Files. *RQ*, 28 (4), 1989, 517-527.

14 SZE, M.C. Serials management with *Inmagic*. *Serials Librarian* 20 (1), 1991, 53-64.

15 WHITE, S. *Inmagic* at Ove Arup. *Vine* 88, September 1992, 22-29.

16 VECCIA, Susan H. *Inmagic Plus* for libraries: it's a library in a box! *Database* 16 (5), October 1993, 44-55.

17 ELLINGEN, Dana C. *Inmagic Plus* – Plus images! *Database* 16 (5), October 1993, 56-59.

18 KERLEY, Peggy N. Litigation technology roundup. *Legal Assistant Today* 11 (1), September 1993, 110-118.

19 GREGORY, Gwen. US Courts Library/Phoenix, develops online catalog using *INMAGIC*. *Information Today* 10 (5), May 1993, 38-39.

20 YORK, Sandra J. An automated solution to the Superfund documentation problem. *Records Management Quarterly* 26 (3), July 1992, 26-28.

21 EDWARDS, Ivana. Simple and inexpensive litigation support on your PC. *Legal Assistant Today* 9 (4), March 1992, 30-43.

22 LEE, Thomas F. Records control in local government using *Inmagic* and *SerchMAGIC* software. *Records Management Quaterly* 26 (1), January 1992, 22-24, 57.

Chapter 2 Importing downloaded records into bibliographic software
Terry Hanson, Head of Research and Information Services, University of Connecticut

The batch importing of records from external databases is the feature which varies most from package to package and presents the user with the greatest problems. In spite of marketing claims to the contrary there are many things that can go wrong. It is also, potentially, the most useful aspect of the software: when the process works smoothly it permits the creation of personal databases in minutes rather than hours or days.

In this chapter we will look at the different possibilities whereby records from a source database can be transferred or 'imported' to a destination bibliographic software package, how each of the packages implements the transfer routines and at the problems and pitfalls involved in the process.

Importing approaches
There are five obvious sources from which records might be imported:
- online databases
- CD-ROM databases
- diskette databases, such as *Current Contents on Diskette*
- online catalogues (OPACs)
- other, mainly database, software packages.

In each case there are three logical possibilities whereby records might make the transfer from source to destination.

These are 'source recognising destination' by providing a suitable download format, 'destination recognising source' by providing a means of reformatting the records and, finally, where an intermediate software package recognises the source and converts to the required format for the destination. We shall look at these possibilities in turn.

Source recognises destination
This is the ideal situation and one for which there is a good precedent. Most company information and statistical databases in all media offer download formats compatible with leading spreadsheets such as *Lotus 1-2-3*. The same feature is needed for bibliographic databases and bibliographic software. At present there are precious few examples of database producers offering bibliographic software compatible download formats.

For compatibility a download format is required that matches the format which the software package uses to store and/or exchange data between its users. No re-formatting should be needed. One solution which any database producer could easily provide is an open, ASCII-based, file format such as the so-called 'comma delimited' ASCII format. This can already be recognised by *dBase4* and *Pro-Cite*. *Pro-Cite* includes, as standard, an 'export' utility to produce records in this format, and an 'import' utility to read them into the destination database. This format enables users of the package to swap records with each other. The CD-ROM citation indexes and *Current Contents on Diskette* databases from ISI offer a *Pro-Cite* compatible download format. *EndNote Plus* can also import these *Pro-Cite* download formats.

Other examples of databases with *Pro-Cite* compatible download formats are the *BITS* diskette service from Biological Abstracts, the forty seven abstracting journals from CAB International are available in *Pro-Cite* format as an alternative to the printed word and, since late 1993, there has been an arrangement between the BLCMP OPAC system and *Pro-Cite*. BLCMP users have the option to download records in *Pro-Cite* comma delimited format either record by record or entire sets resulting from a search. There is a similar relationship between the diskette-based current awareness service *Reference Update* and *Reference Manager* but this is hardly surprising as both are produced by the same company as complementary products.

There are other examples where the source database appears to recognise the destination format but in fact simply offers a download format which can be recognised by the reformatting module of the destination package and are, therefore, an example of the next category.

Destination recognises source: reformatting
The vast majority of downloaded records will find their way into personal bibliographic databases by the reformatting route – if at all. All the packages provide a reformatting utility and they all work in different ways although, in general, they are trying to do the same kind of conversion.

Typically, bibliographic software packages offer this feature for large numbers of external database sources. In *Papyrus* the reformatting utility is built into the package at no extra cost whilst in the others it is purchased separately *(Biblio-Links* for *Pro-Cite, Capture Module* for *Reference Manager* and *EndLink* for *EndNote Plus)*. Either way the packages vary widely in their support for external database sources. There are two important variables:

1   *The method of database recognition*
    Reference Manager and *Papyrus* provide support for individual external databases from a variety of online or CD-ROM sources. *Reference Manager's Capture Module*, for example, recognises 198 mainly biomedical databases, included in which are several versions of *Medline. Papyrus* recognises seventy databases in various subject areas. *EndNote's EndLink* provides recognition via a typical (two character) tagged output modelled on Dialog *Medline* which provides a general, and in most cases far from ideal, recognition for any database which conforms to it.

    The *Pro-Cite* approach is different; it is based upon database hosts and publishers rather than individual databases. There are *Biblio-Links* for Dialog, BRS, STN, Silver Platter, Wilson and Data-Star databases. From early 1994 these hitherto separate packages were integrated into a single package with separate menu options for the different host sources. There is a generic recognition of the host's format (field tags and document headers, etc.) held in a Configuration File. This file also contains individual instructions for each of the databases from that host.

2   *The extent of flexibility and adaptability*
By flexibility and adaptability I am referring to the extent to which it is possible to adapt these reformatting utilities for use with other databases or to modify the process whereby a recognised source is converted.
Pro-Cite and *Papyrus* are very flexible but differ in terms of ease of use and friendliness. *Reference Manager* is not flexible. The whole philosophy of *Reference Manager* appears to be to prevent mistakes being made in the process of data entry. They compensate for the inflexibility of their *Capture Module* by providing formats for unsupported databases at the request of a user and are also site testing a flexible *Capture Module* for release in 1995. *EndLink* already allows its users to create their own import filters for unsupported databases.

Third party reformatting software
In the introduction reference was made to true reformatting software which is both source and destination independent. Such packages are very powerful and, not surprisingly, somewhat more difficult to become familiar with than the reformatting utilities discussed above. Examples of general purpose reformatting software packages include *RefWriter, Filter* and *Headform*. *RefWriter* is the most flexible and powerful of the three.

With these packages the user has a very high degree of control over the various sources that might come along. In addition to reformatting for inclusion in a local database the records might be converted in order to look better when printed or to look better still by having desktop publishing formatting codes embedded.

Reformatting issues and problems
The process of reformatting is one in which many things can go wrong. The possibilities range from records not getting into the destination database at all, through fields and/or sub-fields not being recognised to a perfect conversion. It should be stressed that that despite advertising claims to the contrary no package currently available will accurately and simply convert records from all external databases.

The basic requirements for successful reformatting, apart from consistent and accurate data presentation, are that the source database should have field tags (preferably short and at the beginning of the line, indicating the start of each field), a document header (any string of characters such as the typical Dialog header: 3/4/1, etc.) indicating the start of each record, and something to indicate the end of each record. With these elements in place the reformatting process is simply a matter of deciding which fields from the source are to be imported and to which destination files they should be assigned. It should be straightforward and successful once the basic procedures of the chosen reformatting module have been mastered. Where these elements are not in place there are still possibilities, depending on which package is used, but more ingenuity, dedication and patience are required.

There are two main problem areas.

Separating elements in the downloaded references
One reason why the reformatting process must be as accurate as possible is related to the way the various packages provide output formats for the bibliography when it is ready for printing. Methods of citing documents mainly differ from each other in terms of the punctuation between the different elements of the reference, the order of those field elements and the attributes of the actual text (bold, italic, underlined, or just plain). Consequently, the packages tend to store the records in a very analytical manner with

each separate element of the description being assigned to a separate field. The output formatter can then simply take each field in whichever order is required for a particular style and insert appropriate punctuation in between the fields. This process would break down if, during the reformatting process, data was sent to the wrong field.

The most obvious problem here is when the source database has a single field (e.g. SO or JN) containing the entire journal reference: name, date, volume number, part number, page numbers. The reformatter would then need to have the ability to 'parse' this field in the source database and thus separate out and direct the different elements to the correct fields in the destination database. If this process was not possible then either the records would need manual editing or the output formats would not work as required.

Distinguishing between different document types
Another problem relates to different document types. As all of our packages have different data structures for different document types it is important that imported records arrive at the correct destination data structure. This is likely to be a problem when the source database contains a variety of different document types. If this variety includes books, journals, conference proceedings, theses, etc., then there clearly needs to be a mechanism for recognising the different types in the importing process. This is only likely to be possible if the source database distinguishes between the different document types by including a 'document type' field. Unfortunately this practice is far from universal.

Importing and general purpose text retrieval packages
All the discussion so far about importing records from external databases has been confined to the specialised, personal bibliographic software packages which are the principal focus of this book and which were mainly developed for academic researchers. This raises an interesting paradox. The packages that are targeted at information professionals, the general purpose text retrieval packages described in Chapter 1 (*Inmagic* and *Headfast*, etc.), do not permit

anything like the same degree of potential in this important area. As a result librarians and information professionals of all kinds are increasingly attracted to bibliographic software and the potential it offers for managing bibliographic information both for their own needs as intermediaries and on behalf of their users. The bibliographic software market has, therefore, two distinct camps of users: the information intermediaries and the end-user academic researchers.

It is possible to use general purpose reformatting packages such as *RefWriter* to alter the structure of downloaded records to match that required for a destination database in, say, *Headfast* but perhaps the producers of these packages should think about offering better importing arrangements. *BiB/SEARCH* (a bibliographic software package that appears to have ceased to exist) was, in fact, a general purpose text retrieval package that included pre-defined data structures, output formats and importing arrangements to appeal to a wider audience. Another package, *ideaList*, took a similar approach in its DOS version but not in the later Windows version. *Inmagic* has also made a move in the importing direction by offering two optional modules: the *MARC Adaptor*, for importing US MARC records, and the *Multi-Adaptor*, which is meant as a general purpose reformatter which can be customised for any source but for *Inmagic* only as the destination.

In my opinion the approach which is most likely to be successful will be that which makes fewest demands on the users, regardless of whether those users are academic researchers or information professionals. A small minority of the latter may welcome the opportunity to master the finer points of powerful software like *RefWriter* and *Inmagic* and, having done so, be capable of very impressive results. The majority, however, appear not to have either the time or the inclination to achieve the required level of expertise. Their clear preference is for the customised approach taken in the end-user oriented packages.

As the power and sophistication of the end-user-oriented software increases, narrowing the gap between them and the general purpose packages, the reasons for choosing the latter diminish. There are, of course, applications which require the flexibility of general purpose text retrieval software but often these packages are purchased for straightforward bibliographic database management where downloaded records play an important part. In this area bibliographic software is ideal.

Where librarians can use a single package that will satisfy both their own professional requirements and those of the library's users then that appears to be a popular and successful combination to adopt and promote.

The rest of this book is devoted to case studies on the application of bibliographic and reformatting software packages in six organisations. These will refer to the reasons for choosing the package in the first place, the extent of co-ordination exercised and by whom, the objectives to be achieved and general observations on its use.

Chapter 3 Standardising on *Pro-Cite* at the University of Portsmouth
Terry Hanson, formerly Sub-Librarian, Electronic Information Services, University of Portsmouth

There has been a long standing desire among library staff at the University of Portsmouth (formerly Portsmouth Polytechnic) to find a good quality yet friendly bibliographic software package which they could use in a wide variety of applications and which could be promoted among academic staff for managing their personal files. Since 1984, when microcomputers were first purchased by the Library, this has been seen as an area of computing with enormous potential for individual staff, for academic researchers and for the role and status of the Library in general.

In common with experience at other libraries, staff at Portsmouth have received many requests for information and advice on software for managing personal databases since the advent of microcomputers. This was seen as an obvious application. *Pro-Cite* was discovered in mid 1987 and has been in constant and heavy use ever since throughout the institution, but before this date other, general purpose, packages had been evaluated, and one, *Inmagic*, was used, for a range of library applications and, occasionally, was recommended for use by some academic staff whenever their need was for bibliographic or other text-based database management.

The highly specialised nature of bibliographic software for the academic research market, as indicated in Chapter 1, is such that the potential benefits to researchers are very obvious and compelling. However, it is clear that the majority of academics in most institutions are not yet aware of this, for whatever reason. The view of many academic librarians when they discover such packages is, therefore, to seek to marry the product with the market and to inform their users of the nature and potential of the software. The role of the library in this respect is discussed below.

The objective of the Library at Portsmouth has always been, and still is, to promote the use of bibliographic software among academic staff both as good practice in general and specifically in the interests of supporting the research effort of the institution. In this context it was thought desirable to standardise on the use of a particular package, and to develop information services that would deliver bibliographic information to the user in a format compatible with whatever package was chosen.

A combination of circumstances arose after 1987 which made our ambitious objective look a little more achievable. The principal changes were the arrival of *Pro-Cite*, the increasing availability of microcomputers among academic researchers and the democratisation of access to powerful information retrieval in major bibliographic databases, otherwise known as CD-ROM. The vision was of researchers using CD-ROM databases and downloading records for direct inclusion in their personal databases and of an Electronic Current Awareness Service (ECAS) provided by the Library which would do much of this work for them as far as their regular, predictable information needs were concerned. The ECAS service is described below. Previously, with few computers around, inadequate software and only online databases (with their mediated and costed access) as sources of data, the situation had somewhat less potential.

The role of the library

Attitudes vary as to what role, if any, the library should take to the use of bibliographic software within the parent institution (1). Librarians are seen by many researchers and teachers as the obvious people to consult and it is difficult to think of any good reasons for discouraging this view. It can be seen as an excellent opportunity for librarians and their libraries to raise their profiles within the parent organisations. Institutional computing centres are also seen as potential co-ordinators in this area but libraries, as the principal source of bibliographic information, are much better placed to provide support for users. This question of where responsibility lies is an example of how advances in information storage and delivery technologies are forcing a convergence of roles on libraries and computing centres.

There are four possible responses open to the library:

1 Do nothing, or as little as possible, in the belief that what the academic staff do with their computers is their business. Should there be requests for advice the enquirer would be directed to a software directory or the computing centre.
2 Offer information in the form of a pre-prepared list of packages available with their prices and contact addresses. References to comparative reviews might also be included.
3 Offer information, as above, but with a recommendation. This might be backed up with implicit encouragement to go with the recommended package through price discounts, etc. and perhaps a minimum level of support.
4 Standardise on one package and offer high level support, encouragement and co-ordination. This approach might also incorporate a means of supplying copies of the software to the potential users.

Standardisation

The standardisation route is the most difficult but also, potentially, the most rewarding. The principal advantages are fairly obvious:
- bulk buying discounts through site licences
- support is easier when there is only one package to support
- information interchange is facilitated, in all directions
- electronic current awareness services are possible.

The principal difficulties are:

- how to quickly establish a large user base
- what level of support to provide
- what to do if there is already a variety of packages in use.

Standardisation at Portsmouth

There has been a dual aim at Portsmouth:
- to promote the use of standard bibliographic software and
- to establish an electronic current awareness service.

The Library could fairly claim to have been meeting the first objective by recommending *Pro-Cite* from 1988 onwards and through publicity in the *Polytechnic Bulletin*, specific recommendation, demonstrations and seminars, etc. The existence of *Pro-Cite* became well known but the number of users remained small since the individual concerned had to find the money to obtain a copy from departmental budgets and research grants.

If the second objective was to be achieved it was clear that the user base needed to increase very significantly, and relatively quickly. We decided to make a bid for funding from the Polytechnic's capital funds for a site licence that would enable the Library to give the software to the departments. The only type of site licence then available was for the purchase of full copies complete with documentation. The Library would have preferred a site licence arrangement which allowed unlimited use of *Pro-Cite*, by copying, throughout the institution.

The arrangement that was eventually agreed was based on bulk purchase with substantial discount. The Library put in a bid for sufficient funds to purchase 100 copies with an option to purchase additional copies at a discounted rate of 75 per cent. The bid was successful and the software eventually arrived.

Distribution was based on the number of academic staff in departments and in the context of the announcement that an Electronic Current Awareness Service (ECAS) would be launched at the same time. This was in July 1990. Since then further copies have been purchased by the departments at substantial discounts and in January 1994 the number of copies in use was approximately 230.

Chapter 3

Why *Pro-Cite?*
Before describing ECAS it is perhaps of interest to consider the reasons for the choice of *Pro-Cite*. There are many end-user-oriented bibliographic software packages on the market now that would meet our requirements of ease of use and appropriate features. The package chosen had to appeal to staff and students in a multi-disciplinary institution in terms of its pre-defined data structures and output formats and, very importantly, in terms of its importing arrangements. It also had to be a package which was well supported and, preferably, widely used.

Without wishing to undertake an exhaustive comparative review, it was clear that *Pro-Cite* succeeded on all counts. It offers twenty input formats which include the normal books and journal articles plus other types of publication and various audio-visual materials. There are thirty output formats based on the requirements of particular journals and organisations (plus the ability to create others). In terms of importing from external databases *Pro-Cite* scores very highly for its flexibility. The various *Biblio-Links* cover most major online hosts and, more recently, Silver Platter and Wilson CD-ROM databases also. Further, arrangements are well under way for a *Pro-Cite* compatible download format from the OPAC of the BLCMP library system used at Portsmouth. The only major weakness of *Pro-Cite* at the time it was chosen was its slow searching speed. The search technique was not one based on conventional indexes as used by all the other packages discussed in Chapter 1. Instead *Pro-Cite* looked at each record in sequence for the required search term(s). However, in version 2, launched in 1992, the shortcoming disappeared and the search speed is now very fast.

Reference Manager and *BiB/SEARCH* were also considered. The former was considered too specialised in its biomedical orientation and insufficiently adaptable, although otherwise excellent, while the latter was not considered friendly enough for use by novices.

Another consideration was the needs of Library staff and more advanced users. Flexibility was required to allow, for example, the automatic formatting of structured bibliographies (organised by subject keywords, etc.), the importing of records from a very wide variety of sources and the writing of non-standard output formats such as the document request form described below. *Reference Manager* does not allow this degree of flexibility.

Finally, it was more important in terms of Library strategy that a standard was established than it was to choose the objectively 'perfect' package. There were considerable advantages to be gained from acting in a clear and well co-ordinated way to bring a single, good quality, package to the attention of the academic community before they discovered a wide variety of different ones, of varying quality, for themselves. Libraries embarking on this course now may find that awareness of bibliographic software among the academic staff has indeed complicated the situation. Certainly there has been a strong advertising campaign aimed directly at researchers through appropriate journals and a range of articles written for end-user consumption (see the bibliography at the end of the book).

The Electronic Current Awareness Service (2, 3)
Traditional current awareness services in academic libraries are derived from a limited range of local sources in broad subject areas and delivered to groups of people, e.g. departments, etc. The ECAS service is very different. Its information comes from very large – near comprehensive – sources, caters for specific subjects and is delivered to individuals. It is a tailored information service which takes references from major bibliographic databases regardless of media (CD-ROM, online, diskette or the local OPAC) and delivers them in electronic form to users for inclusion in their personal *Pro-Cite* databases. Updates can be delivered at intervals ranging from a week to three months.

The CD-ROM and diskette databases are the most important sources since the Library subscribes to about twenty CD-ROM databases and the whole range of *Current Contents on Diskette* products. Unlike SDIs stored on online databases there are no connect charges involved in running regular

Chapter 3

searches but the suitability of CD-ROM and diskette databases varies considerably. Three features are essential if they are to be used in this way.

1. It should be possible to identify the records in the source database that were added in the most recent update since these are the only records which require searching. This does not apply to the diskette databases (such as *Current Contents on Diskette*) which are issued weekly as separate databases but is very important for cumulative CD-ROM databases. The majority of these sources do not permit this very obvious task to be accomplished.
2. The storage and reuse of search profiles or strategies should be permitted. This is important for reasons of time (some profiles are very long and it would be tedious to have to type them in every time they needed to be run) and accuracy (there is obviously plenty of scope for typing mistakes).
3. It must be possible to import the downloaded references into *Pro-Cite*. The possibilities here include the ideal, whereby the source database offers a download format specifically compatible with the chosen package, and the normal situation which requires some reformatting.

On all three counts the ISI databases on CD-ROM and diskette score highly. Silver Platter has recently introduced Search History storage on its CD-ROM but it is very weak on the identification of new records with only *PsycLIT* and *Medline* offering this possibility. The *Silver Platter Biblio-Link* routines work very well on the recognised databases. Some vendors, such as UMI, make life difficult on all three counts. The majority of the eighty or so current profiles at Portsmouth are for use with the *Current Contents on Diskette* products and are delivered to the users weekly.

A recent enhancement (February 1993) to the ECAS service involves monthly updates of additions to the Library's book stock. Each month all new book records are downloaded from the BLCMP catalogue database and converted to *Pro-Cite* format. Within *Pro-Cite*, search profiles (expressions) are created using either keywords or Dewey class numbers. The profiles are stored and run each month with output for users in either *Pro-Cite* format or laser printed in class number order. This has proved a very popular addition to the service with more than 100 applications in the first two months of operation.

The work of running the ECAS service is divided between Subject Librarians and clerical assistants. The former have the responsibility of liaising with academic staff, promoting the service, working out the profiles and deciding which databases need to be searched. Once the profile has been stored the job is handed over to the clerical staff. It is their task to run the profile at the desired frequency, to download the retrieved references and to deliver the file(s) by diskette to the user. If reformatting is necessary then they have been trained to run these routines also.

Finally, a retrospective service is also offered whereby a major search over many years is done to establish a personal database. For this purpose the local online catalogue would be used in addition to online and CD-ROM sources.

Level of support
Once the decision is made to standardise on a bibliographic software package then it follows that there must be an appropriate level of support if the standard is to be 'maintained'. This can place a considerable burden on the Library but the benefits to users are considerable and the Library is seen to be fulfilling an important new role in the university.

The forms of support at Portsmouth include:

The provision of the software through the site licence
This covers the initial supply (free of charge) and the supply of upgrades. Departments may purchase extra copies of the software at a heavily discounted rate and individual staff can purchase copies for private use.

Current awareness
The ECAS service encourages use of *Pro-Cite*. The

motivation to use it would be reduced if all the references had to be typed in manually.

Publicity
This is achieved by the distribution of a leaflet advertising the service, by writing about it in the *Polytechnic Bulletin* and in departmental bulletins, by staff seminars and demonstrations and by word of mouth whenever bibliographic databases are discussed.

Training workshops
There are on average four workshops for staff each term lasting three hours and covering the basics of manual data entry, importing, printing, searching and merging.

Pocket guide
This is a short guide to the use of *Pro-Cite* which covers all the basic functions and which refers to ECAS arrangements.

Consultation and advice
All Subject Librarians have taken on a support role for staff in their departments.

Document requests
As part of the ECAS service the Library provides a special *Pro-Cite* output format file, known as a Punctuation File, which prints selected records from the personal database as application forms for either inter library loans or photocopies from Library stock. Thus the ECAS user can follow up the references provided each week with the minimum of effort.

Student and administrative use
The main focus has been academic staff and researchers since they are clearly the principal gatherers of bibliographic information but efforts have also been made to encourage students and administrative staff to use *Pro-Cite*.

Students
It is not expected that many students will wish to buy their

own copy of the software, although some have expressed interest. The hope is that they will avail themselves of it on public machines located in their departments and in the Library. To encourage this a series of exercises has been jointly developed with the departments which require the students to compile a selective bibliography on a chosen subject, provide annotations indicating reasons for inclusion and present the work as a *Pro-Cite* database. To assist them the students are given a standard training workshop in small groups. This combines three separate learning objectives. The students learn something about the subject under examination, they learn about the process of gathering bibliographic information from appropriate sources and their information technology skills are reinforced through the use of a computer software package.

Administrative staff
In promoting *Pro-Cite* to researchers library staff have also emphasised its potential for administrative support in academic departments. Secretarial staff are constantly called upon to type bibliographies and reading lists. This task can be managed much more efficiently with *Pro-Cite* than a word processor. Many departments realised this and arranged for their administrative staff to be trained; others were a little slower in making the connection.

A major step forward was taken early in 1993 when the Library proposed that *Pro-Cite* be used to establish and maintain a University publications database. Each year every department submits to the Library a *Pro-Cite* database of their staff publications. The combined database is checked for bibliographic details and indexed using several classification criteria. It is then made available to all who need to use it. This necessitated a new training programme specifically for administrative support staff which concentrates on the procedures they need to use most.

Other administrative uses include the management of relatively small collections of material in special units. Examples include video and audio tapes in the Languages Department and all published materials in the Academic

Development Centre and in the Centre for the Management of Aquatic Resources (Cemare).

Conclusion

The University Library has taken a major initiative in establishing an institutional standard for bibliographic database software and promoting it among academic staff throughout the institution. This, and the establishment of the Electronic Current Awareness Service, has proved to be very popular and has been of great benefit to the staff of the institution and to the role and standing of the Library.

There is no doubt that the use of bibliographic software by academic researchers throughout the world will grow as access to the major bibliographic databases improves and microcomputers are used for more and more purposes. Two points follow from this.

1. The producers of databases – in whatever physical format – and their publishers or vendors will have to offer appropriate download formats compatible with the leading software packages. This will allow end-users to download references and import them directly into their personal databases.
2. Libraries in universities – and elsewhere – will be called upon to distribute bibliographic information to researchers in software compatible formats. This information may be the product of one-off online searches or it may be part of a full-blown electronic current awareness service (as at Portsmouth).

The library will find its role much more manageable if it attempts to co-ordinate the use of bibliographic software throughout the institution and restrict the number of packages in use, preferably to one. From the library's point of view it is much better to anticipate these developments rather than wait until the users force the issue.

References

1 HANSON, T. Libraries, universities and bibliographic software. *British Journal of Academic Librarianship* 7 (1), 1992, 45-54.

2 DOHERTY, F.J. and FARQUHAR, I.K. *Pro-Cite, EndNote* and *Reference Manager. Computer Applications in the Biosciences* 7 (1), 1991, 128-132.

3 FRANCIS, J.L. *Reference Manager* version 5. *Blood Coagulation and Fibrinolysis* 2 (4), 1991, 577-578.

Chapter 4 Library support for *Reference Manager* at a School of Medicine
John Cox, Information Services, Wellcome Centre for Medical Science (formerly at Royal Free Hospital School of Medicine)

This chapter begins by describing the need for bibliographic software at the Royal Free Hospital School of Medicine and outlining the reasons why *Reference Manager* (1-6) was selected as the standard package for bibliographic data management. Further sections examine the strengths and weaknesses of the package, in our experience, and the role of the Medical Library in promoting the adoption of *Reference Manager* and in supporting its use. Finally, some of the ways in which the software has been used to support the Library's information services are described.

Why bibliographic software?
The main impetus for the widespread adoption of bibliographic software at the Royal Free was provided by the advent of easy access to bibliographic data in electronic, more specifically CD-ROM, format. When we introduced a CD-ROM search service, based on the *Medline* database initially, in June 1989 the service proved extremely popular with library users. It also highlighted the need for the Medical Library to take an active role in assisting users with problems of information management resulting from the retrieval and downloading of large quantities of bibliographic data. Users began to realise that CD-ROM searches could be a mixed blessing if the references retrieved merely took the

form of a collection of lengthy printouts or of a series of files stored on one or more floppy disks. The ability to retrieve specific data from these collections was clearly limited without the facility to store references in personal databases which could be easily created and searched with bibliographic software.

Medical school and hospital staff publish more than 1,000 journal articles and conference papers each year. Citation of previous contributions to the literature is prominent in medical papers and it was evident that software which could directly generate bibliographies of papers whose records had been downloaded from electronic databases would save time in the research and publication processes. Awareness of the capabilities of bibliographic software packages was increasing as a result of promotional literature and discussions with colleagues elsewhere.

Not surprisingly the Medical Library began to receive regular enquiries about bibliographic software from users anxious to find a way to manage the flood of data in electronic format and to re-use this data in their publications. We recognised the need to provide expertise in co-ordinating the use of bibliographic software. Our objective was to take the lead role in establishing one package as the standard at the Royal Free and to promote and support its use. We were also motivated by the opportunity which the widespread adoption of bibliographic software would afford for the development of new information services, especially to satisfy a demand from users for improved current awareness.

Why *Reference Manager?*

The conventional approach in selecting software is to conduct a detailed examination of a number of rival packages and to choose the one which offers the best combination of features and the fewest weaknesses. In this respect the Royal Free's experience is untypical. One look at *Reference Manager*, the first bibliographic software package examined, was sufficient to convince us that this was a package which the Medical Library could recommend to its users and for which we could offer full technical support. Subsequent experience has confirmed this impression.

Two general features particularly commended *Reference Manager*: its specifically biomedical orientation and its ease of use. This software was designed *by* a biomedical researcher *for* biomedical researchers. As a result it allows records to be imported from a wide range of medical databases in online, CD-ROM and floppy disk format. The biomedical bias is also reflected in the predefined data output formats which can be purchased with the package. These formats enable bibliographies to be generated in the styles required for the submission of manuscripts to over 140 journals (now 185), most of which are in medical fields. The relevance of *Reference Manager* to our users' needs was, therefore, immediately obvious. The increasing popularity of this package among researchers at other medical schools and hospitals in Britain and internationally was also significant. Its adoption at the Royal Free would facilitate the sharing of data in collaborative research with other organisations and could also provide an element of future-proofing for users when moving to other jobs.

Simplicity is bliss, especially for a small medical library aiming to provide comprehensive technical support for bibliographic software among a user population of modest computer literacy. At the time we were introducing *Reference Manager* our users were only beginning to get to grips with the application of microcomputers for more complex tasks than word processing. Their priorities were patient care and medical research rather than mastery of the intricacies of operating systems or programming. As a Library we had recently implemented a heavily used CD-ROM search service and were introducing new equipment and procedures for office automation. Other computerisation projects were planned in the near future. The amount of time which could be given to supporting bibliographic software would, therefore, be limited.

Our priority was to standardise on a package which would be simple to install and use, capable of performing a limited number of basic routines quickly and efficiently and be robust when regularly used by individuals with varying experience of computing and bibliographic data management. *Reference Manager*, as explained below, seemed well suited to our needs.

Strengths
Ease of use is the overriding impression given by a demonstration of *Reference Manager*. Our experience at the Royal Free has shown that this feature endures in the more critical context of actual use, often by researchers working to tight deadlines and still in the process of familiarising themselves fully with the software.

The basic processes of data entry and importation, retrieval and bibliography generation are clearly presented on the main menu. All procedures are menu-driven and user help, although rarely needed, is available at the touch of the F1 function key.

The manual provided with the software is generally clear, the most useful section being the second chapter in which the new user is taken through a tutorial of the main features. The tutorial uses a sample database which is supplied to all purchasers and automatically created as part of the recommended installation procedure. It is anticipated that the user will rarely need to consult the manual again after the tutorial. This can be interpreted either as a mark of confidence in the straightforward nature of the software or a recognition of the aversion which medical researchers appear to display towards all computer manuals!

It is worth examining the operation of the basic functions of the software in more depth.

Capture Module
From my point of view the most valuable feature is the Capture Module which automatically reformats data from a wide range of medical databases into the proprietary record structure employed by *Reference Manager*. Given the varied structure of records from different databases or from the same databases when loaded by different hosts or CD-ROM publishers, automatic conversion to the required structure is vital. The reformatting procedure is transparent to the user

and works in the same way whether records are taken from *Medline, PSYCINFO, EMBASE* or *Current Contents on Diskette*. It is, therefore, easy to create personal databases from many different sources.

Of equal significance *Medline* records from more than fifteen different online or CD-ROM sources can be captured. This is helpful to users who move to or from organisations which offer different versions of *Medline*, e.g. CD Plus or SilverPlatter. It is also important for libraries which, given the competitive nature of the marketplace for *Medline* in compact disc format, may consider changing to a different CD-ROM publisher at some future point.

A final point to make regarding data reformatting is that as a small library we are not in a position to commit time to devising word processor macros, for instance, to convert records to the required structure. We therefore appreciate the inclusion of most of our major source databases in the Capture Module and the willingness of Research Information Systems Inc., publishers of *Reference Manager*, to incorporate new sources on request.

Bibliography generation
This is the most appealing feature as far as the busy researcher is concerned. The formatting of manuscripts to fit the various styles required by medical journals has long been seen as a tedious job which consumes valuable research time. The researcher's frustration is compounded when a manuscript is rejected by one journal and has to be reformatted when submitted to another. The needs of the researcher in this respect are very well catered for by *Reference Manager* which takes care of the routine work while the researcher concentrates on the intellectual input.

As mentioned earlier, an optional module contains the codes necessary to reformat *Reference Manager* records into the styles required by more than 185 journals. The procedure is straightforward for the user whose sole concern is to select the necessary references to be cited from the database. This process is simplified by *Reference Manager*'s Splicer Module which allows pop-up access to the database from within the user's word processor while the manuscript is being composed. Any required references are marked and their database ID numbers are automatically inserted, with a special delimiter, in the manuscript at the appropriate point. The user then nominates the appropriate journal style, after which the software will search the manuscript for the cited record ID numbers and produce a bibliography with all the necessary punctuation and typefaces. *Reference Manager* is compatible with a range of word processors, notably *Word* and *Word for Windows, WordPerfect, Ami Pro* and *WordStar*, and will generate the bibliography accordingly. All in-text citations (e.g. super-scripted numbers (23) or authors and years (Smith, 1983)) are also provided. Any new journal format can be created easily by copying and editing an existing one.

Retrieval facilities
Among the other strengths of *Reference Manager* which have been commented upon by users are its straightforward and powerful retrieval facilities. Searching is entirely menu-driven, the user being presented with a list of fields to search and prompted for the appropriate Boolean operator. The main search fields are author, subject keyword, journal name, publication year, title word(s) or title/abstract word(s). The first four fields are all indexed, giving the searcher two advantages. Searching of indexed fields is extremely fast, indeed almost instantaneous, even in large databases.

Retrieval is made simpler and more comprehensive by the ready availability of look-up lists of, for instance, all authors or journal names in any database. The searcher can select terms directly from these lists, thus reducing the amount of typing involved. All of the look-up lists are accessible during manual entry of records also and can be used to ensure that author names and journal titles are uniform throughout a databases and that keywords are consistently applied. The saving of typing effort is even more welcome at this point.

Reprint management
Provision is also made for efficient reprint management. Each record contains a field in which the user can indicate whether a copy of the original document is in file, on request or not in file. The date of application is automatically assigned to items on request and these can be searched through the Pending Reprint option on the retrieval menu. Some users will still experience the frustration of being informed by *Reference Manager* that a particular item is in file but being unable to locate it amid the mass of paper strewn about the office or laboratory! Not surprisingly, however, many users have begun to organise their reprint collections more efficiently in order to take full advantage of the facilities offered by their bibliographic software. One easy way of doing this is to file all reprints according to the running number assigned by the software to identify each item uniquely. If an existing filing system is already in place another possibility is to add the relevant filing code as a keyword.

Weaknesses
The flipside of *Reference Manager*'s simplicity is its inflexibility. The program has a number of limitations which, while they have rarely caused problems at the Royal Free, might seriously compromise its value in other organisations. At the heart of these limitations is the biomedical orientation of the software. Nowhere is this more evident than in the vital area of data importation from other databases.

Inflexibility of the Capture Module
A look at the list of sources from which data are automatically reformatted by the Capture Module reveals an almost exclusive emphasis on biomedical databases. There are one or two exceptions, notably the Dialog versions of the engineering databases *Compendex Plus* and *Inspec*. Nevertheless, users of business information, for example, would find little support for their databases. Research Information Systems Inc. would do well to consider expanding the scope of the Capture Module to take its

considerable benefits to non-medical users.

Even medical users sometimes experience frustration with the Capture Module in its present form. There is at present no facility for users to define their own import formats for automatically importing records from databases not included in this Module. One solution is to devise a word processor macro to convert downloaded data into a format accepted by *Reference Manager*. A flexible Capture Module which can be customised by the user to support new databases is promised for 1995.

An alternative approach is to send a representative sample of downloaded records to Research Information Systems. The company is always willing to add new source databases to the Capture Module, provided the database is well known. The requester is not charged, although other users are expected to pay for updates of this Module.

Input formats
Research Information Systems have recently expressed a commitment to making the software attractive to users outside the biomedical field and this development is welcome. Version 6, for example, allows more than thirty types of references to be included in a database. Previously this number was only six, reflecting the most common types of medical publications. There is now a field for issue number as well as volume number in the journal article reference type. Earlier versions made provision only for volume number since medical journals do not usually require an issue number to be cited. Page numbers are sequential throughout a volume (i.e. each separate issue does not begin on page one as in many other disciplines) so it is sufficient to cite volume and page number only.

Size limitation on databases
Our users have frequently queried one of *Reference Manager*'s more surprising limitations. Purchasers of the program are allowed to create only one database of more than 200 references. This database can, however, be as large as 65,000 records for purchasers of the RM Professional

version of the software. Most of our users have bought this version and have, reluctantly in some cases, adapted to the need to concentrate on one major database. It is possible to create any number of smaller databases for other purposes but their size is always confined to 200 records in the long term, although users are permitted to exceed this limit temporarily. Some users, myself included, would naturally like to have the flexibility to create a series of large databases. Indeed, it is hard to see the justification for imposing such a limitation when users have paid more than £200 for their copy of the software. Research Information Systems argue that illegal copying of the software is prevented by limiting each copy of *Reference Manager* to a single major database. One can sympathise with this point of view but the restriction imposed is still frustrating to the bona fide purchaser.

Library support
From the outset we were determined that the Medical Library should take the lead role in promoting and providing full technical support for the use of *Reference Manager*, a role for which we felt well equipped through our familiarity with computers and bibliographic data. We recognised the importance of actively establishing a local standard rather than passively watching our users purchase a range of software of varying quality in which our limited staffing resources would not allow us to develop any expertise (7).

Bulk purchase of software
Apart from the quality of the software a further incentive towards standardising on *Reference Manager* was the application of a 40 per cent discount (now 30 per cent) to an initial bulk order for twenty copies and of 30 per cent (now 20 per cent) to all subsequent orders throughout the next year. As a result of a concentrated promotional effort we were able to raise an order for twenty six copies within five weeks. All the administrative work involved in processing these orders was handled by the Library which has continued to perform this co-ordinating role during the past eighteen months while

the number of copies purchased has grown to more than eighty.

Technical support
Our aim has always been to do far more than simply promote the adoption of *Reference Manager*, however. Technical support for the software is an activity to which the Library has devoted considerable time and effort. This support takes a variety of forms, beginning with the installation of the software on the user's microcomputer. This saves time for the user and provides an opportunity for a quick overview of *Reference Manager*'s main functions and how they work.

Bearing in mind the reluctance of users to digest the content of the manual properly, the Library has produced some supplementary sheets of documentation. One of these takes the form of a series of questions and answers and addresses some of the most common queries raised by users concerning aspects such as word processor and printer compatibility, procedures for importing data from commonly used databases and the permitted size of *Reference Manager* databases. Other sheets illustrate the stages involved in creating a manuscript bibliography and in making backup copies of any databases. Some of our users have learned the value of the information contained in the latter sheet through bitter experience!

Advisory service
Ongoing support is available through an advisory service which means that help can be obtained by a telephone call or a visit to the Library. Through this service we are able to identify recurrent problems which we report to Research Information Systems, although the majority of enquiries can be dealt with locally.

It may be of interest to note that the source of most problems can be found at the data entry or importation stage. Databases can become corrupted through untidy or incomplete manual entry of records, for instance. More commonly, corruption can result from the selection of the wrong import format. A typical example is the attempt to use

Chapter 4

the BRS online *Medline* format to import records from the SilverPlatter CD-ROM version of this database. Unfortunately, despite our attempts to anticipate such problems in the local documentation we provide, end users are often unaware that *Medline* exists in many different guises. The result of the erroneous selection mentioned here is that data from a number of records will be imported with scrambled punctuation after which the software will crash, presenting the user with a cryptic error message.

Another regular source of difficulties is the importation of records in a non-ASCII format. It is not surprising to find that word processor codes are not well received by *Reference Manager*!

Information services

The widespread adoption of a bibliographic database package in the medical school and hospital has opened up opportunities for the Library to develop new information services. Foremost among these is our electronic current awareness service, Current Awareness on Disk (8).

Current Awareness on Disk.

When we introduced a CD-ROM search service, based on *Medline*, our users were quick to note that the latest references in their subject areas were not being retrieved and that time lags between publication of articles and their appearance in the database often ranged from three to six months or more. At around the same time, mid-1989, the *Current Contents on Diskette* series had recently become available. This series is delivered at weekly intervals on floppy disk, thus offering a more up-to-date source of references in electronic format than *Medline* on CD-ROM (9). Indeed the time lag for references is typically between two and six weeks. Since *Current Contents* records can be imported into *Reference Manager* automatically via the Capture Module the potential clearly existed for the Library to provide a weekly electronic current awareness service to its users.

Our service is largely based on the *Life Sciences* and *Social and Behavioral Sciences* editions of *Current Contents on Diskette*. The user nominates a search profile which is run each week by the Library. The results are output in a format which has been specially designed for users of *Reference Manager* by the publishers of *Current Contents on Diskette*. These records are copied to a floppy disk and mailed to the user whose only task is to read the file within *Reference Manager*, add important references to the personal database or reject them as appropriate, and return the disk to the Library for the next weekly update by reversing the address label on the envelope.

As a result the user is able at the same time to keep up to date and to build a personal database of references on subjects of interest. The value of such a service would be greatly diminished without *Reference Manager* which provides a simple means of controlling the flow of data and retaining it in electronic format for later retrieval and re-use.

The *Current Awareness on Disk* service also generates valuable income for the Library which is used towards expanding our electronic information services (7, 10). We make a small charge of £25 or £35 a year to each user of the service. The cost is kept low deliberately to encourage take-up and the service now has more than fifty users, generating over £1,800 annually. We also support the service by photocopying, at a higher charge than for self-service copying, articles from weekly searches which are stocked by the Library and requested by the user.

Database of staff publications
The Library's other main use of *Reference Manager* for information services is in the compilation of a database of Royal Free staff publications. For some time the task of producing a list of departmental publications specifically for inclusion in the medical school's annual report had been the Library's responsibility. This involved a lot of effort, including manual entry of data into a database which was set up using *Inmagic* software. *Inmagic* is a fairly complex package, requiring considerable effort to set up different import and export formats for bibliographic data.

The application of *Reference Manager* to this task has

simplified it greatly, enabling records of Royal Free publications to be imported directly from a range of online, CD-ROM and floppy disk databases. The database is now updated on an ongoing rather than an annual basis and contains more than 5,000 records. In addition to generating the annual list of publications from the database we can also produce up-to-date lists at any time and in any format for individuals or departments on request.

Training of students
Some use of *Reference Manager* has also been made in practical sessions run by the Library for students as part of an information technology course devised by the medical school's Department of Medical Computing and Informatics. This is likely to be a growth area in the future as the need to provide training at the earliest opportunity in the major applications of computers in medicine becomes more widely recognised. Information retrieval and management have long been seen as vital skills for medical professionals (11) and we see an important role for the Library in ensuring that the potential of bibliographic software in medicine is fully realised and exploited.

Conclusion
The adoption of *Reference Manager* as the standard package for bibliographic data management has significantly benefited the Library and its users. Despite a number of limitations this software has proved ideal for our needs, its major assets of simplicity, speed and medical focus far outweighing some inflexibility and restrictions on database size. The availability of a Windows version (*WinRM*) and the recent introduction of the *Reference Manager Network Edition* offer further advantages.

The processes of research and publication have been made more efficient by the powerful facilities offered by the package for data importation, retrieval and re-use in manuscript bibliographies. The *Current Awareness on Disk* service has enabled users to keep up to date with the literature more easily than before and at the same time generated significant revenue for further development of the Library's electronic information services.

A final point to note is that the image of the Library and its status in the organisation as a whole have definitely been enhanced by the role taken in promoting and supporting the software and by the new services which it has enabled us to provide to our users.

References

1   COX, J. *Reference Manager* version 5.01 for MS-DOS. *Health Libraries Review* 8 (2), 1991, 108-110.

2   DOHERTY, F.J. and FARQUHAR, I.K. *Pro-Cite, EndNote, Reference Manager. Computer Applications in the Biosciences* 7 (1), 1991, 128-132.

3   FRANCIS, J.L. *Reference Manager* version 5.0. *Blood Coagulation and Fibrinolysis* 2 (4), 1991, 577-578.

4   LUNDEEN, G. Bibliographic software update. *Database* 14 (6), 1991, 57-67.

5   LUNDEEN, G. Software for managing personal files. *Database* 12 (3), 1989, 36-48.

6   MATUS, N. and BEUTLER, E.B. *Reference Update* and *Reference Manager*: personal computer programs for locating and managing references. *BioTechniques* 7 (6), 1989, 636-639.

7   COX, J. Making your electronic information products promote and pay for each other. In: *Online information 91. Proceedings of the 15th International Online Information Meeting, 10-12 December 1991*. Edited by D. I. Raitt, Learned Information, 1991, 421-428.

8   COX, J. and HANSON, T. Setting up an electronic current awareness service. *Online* 16 (4), 1992, 36-43.

9 DAWSON, K., COX, J. and SMITH, O. Computer-based knowledge systems. *Lancet* 339, 1992, 185-186.

10 COX, J. and FLETCHER, A. Using new electronic information products to fund others. *Health Libraries Review* 8 (2), 1991, 87-93.

11 GOLDEN, W.E. and FRIEDLANDER, I.R. Development of a pre-printed medical literature filing system. *Journal of Medical Education* 61 (5), 1986, 416-418.

Chapter 5 *EndNote* on the Mac at the Imperial Cancer Research Fund
Jane Milligan, Systems Librarian, Imperial Cancer Research Fund

The Imperial Cancer Research Fund is one of Europe's major cancer research charities, with an income in 1992-93 of over £55 million. It employs over 1,000 research staff, who are engaged in both laboratory-based and clinical research. ICRF's work is spread across multiple sites, with our main laboratories in Lincoln's Inn Fields, in central London, a second laboratory site at South Mimms in Hertfordshire, and research groups on ten other sites in London, seven in Oxford, Cambridge, Bristol, Leeds, Edinburgh and Dundee. The research groups can vary from a single small team to a number of large laboratories.

Computing facilities
At present the central facilities at Lincoln's Inn Fields consist of a cluster of two VAX 8700s for research work, plus other machines for administration, although it is intended to transfer to a Unix-based system running on DEC Alphas during 1994. There has been much investment in desktop computing, with most researchers using Apple Macs, although there are also a number of PC users and increasing use of Sun workstations.

Most of the local sites have local area networks (LANs), mainly using Ethernet, and these LANs are linked to the central computing facilities by a wide area network,

Chapter 5

ICRFNET. This uses leased BT kilostream lines with the LANS connected by routers. In addition to our own network we have connections to JANET and the Internet.

Library and Information Services
The main Library is at Lincoln's Inn Fields with a branch Library at South Mimms. There are ten full time, and two part time staff, based in the main Library but serving all sites. The major services provided are:
- photocopying from our own stock for researchers based away from the central laboratories
- inter-library loans for all staff
- online literature searches: the most commonly used database is Data-Star *Medline*
- CD-ROM databases: in particular, both libraries offer SilverPlatter *Medline* and a number of other sites have their own subscriptions
- current awareness which is provided from the *SciSearch* source tapes processed using the *BasisPlus* text retrieval software on the VAX cluster
- in-house databases, also using *BasisPlus*, including: a two-year cumulation of *SciSearch* data, inter-library loan requests, book and journal catalogues, staff publications and full text of the annual *Scientific Report* (1)
- end-user access via JANET or the Internet to external databases such as the BIDS service.

Bibliographic software
Our initial investigation of personal bibliographic software was begun mainly as a result of a growing number of enquiries from our users. Some were simply aware of a need to manage their ever-expanding reference collections, others had had experience of software elsewhere or had seen advertisements for various packages. In addition, two developments in Library services meant that we were increasingly able to provide bibliographic data in an electronic format.

Firstly, we were encouraging users to change from paper printouts to E-mail, as a means of receiving the results of online and current awareness (CAS) searches. For CAS in

57

particular, this saves a lot of staff time in distribution, not to mention a number of trees! It also provides faster, more reliable delivery to our scattered locations.

Secondly came the launch at ICRF of *Medline* on CD-ROM and the chance to download search results to floppy disks as well as printing them. Later, downloading facilities became available with our own in-house databases and, more recently, from the BIDS service.

As our users began to accumulate computer files of bibliographic data, they naturally wanted to know what they could do with them, other than just produce printouts or save the files in a word processor. How could they store and use their files effectively?

Software review

To answer their questions I carried out a survey of available software, in the summer of 1989. Being an institution heavily biased towards Macs, the choice at that time was very limited. I identified three products which might be suitable and obtained copies for trial use. These were:
- *EndNote*
- *Pro-Cite*
- *Reference Manager*.

After experimenting with these, I produced a paper for enquirers outlining the facilities to look for in bibliographic software and comparing the features of each of the three trial programs. At this stage we did not feel it was appropriate for the Library to make a specific recommendation of which to select. Each had different strengths and weaknesses and suitability depended on the needs of the individual user.

Moreover, at this stage it was not clear whether the Library or the Central Computer Unit should take responsibility for recommending and supporting the software. In the event, *EndNote* very rapidly became the 'consumer choice' and, as a result, the Computer Unit made a discount purchase agreement in the summer of 1991 (on the basis that ICRF would acquire a total of 30 - 50 copies in the course of a year).

Why EndNote?
Why did *EndNote* become so popular so quickly?
- it was the cheapest!
- it had been written for the Mac, not developed from a PC product, and looked most like other Mac software; in the Mac environment, most programs have been designed to have a very similar 'look and feel'
- users generally found it very easy to learn and use
- it offered more flexibility than *Reference Manager*, such as in the variety of data types available, yet was more straightforward to use than *Pro-Cite*
- it was particularly good for linking to a word processor, to produce bibliographies and in-text references which appeared to be the prime concern of many users
- it was the only one which could be run as a 'desk accessory' simultaneously with a word processing program which made it easy to 'cut and paste' references into the text
- it offered very flexible and generally reliable data loading via the *EndLink* module
- in particular, at that time it was the only one which could accept the *Medline* formats from both Data-Star and SilverPlatter

It should be noted that these comparisons applied to the versions available in late 1989; there has been substantial development of all the programs since then.

EndNote itself has undergone a number of changes. It is now available for PC users as well as Mac and has a substantially revised version known as *EndNote Plus* which is used by most people at ICRF. With the advent of Microsoft *Word* version 5, the *EndNote Plus* package now includes a 'plug-in module' for *Word*. Simply by copying the module into the 'Word Commands' folder, *EndNote* becomes an option on *Word*'s Tools Menu, and can be used almost as if it were part of the *Word* software.

***EndNote Plus* and Library services**

At present the Library can offer *EndNote Plus* users a variety of data in electronic form, to load into their databases or process as they wish.

Current awareness
As noted above, our Current Awareness Service (CAS) is provided from *SciSearch* tapes, loaded into a *BasisPlus* database. Tapes are received and processed weekly and searches are run for nearly 400 users. Up to 1994, abstracts were not included in CAS outputs, printed or electronic, as we feared they would make the files very large although they were loaded to the cumulative database.In February 1994 we started trials of both searching and supplying abstracts with the CAS service.

Those who wish can:
- receive their weekly file via E-mail on the VAX cluster
- edit the file to remove unwanted items
- copy the edited file into our automated request system for photocopies or inter-library loans
- automatically pick up the related abstracts from the *SciSearch* database, if not sent with the CAS
- transfer the file to their Mac and load into *EndNote*.

SciSearch database
Originally our *SciSearch* database held the last six months of data (we did not have enough disk space to hold a longer period). From January 1994 the database has been upgraded to hold the last two years' data. It can be searched using an easy menu interface and the results of searches can be either passed directly to the requests system or saved as a VAX file for printing or transfer to *EndNote Plus*.

Both *SciSearch* and CAS use a downloading format which has been set up to mimic Data-Star *Medline* for consistency with literature search results.

Literature searches
Literature searches are carried out by Library staff on behalf of our users via the VAX cluster and JANET. The results of searches can be E-Mailed, edited, requested, transferred to the Mac and stored in *EndNote Plus*.

Medline on CD
SilverPlatter *Medline* is available in both Libraries and at

Chapter 5

ten other sites. The results of searches can be saved onto floppy disks, transferred to the user's own machine and loaded to *EndNote Plus*.

BIDS ISI Database
ICRF also shares in a CHEST cluster subscription to the BIDS ISI service. Results of BIDS searches can be E-mailed directly to the user for loading to *EndNote*. (See note below).

EndNote Plus and the users

EndNote Plus is now being used by many of the laboratories and units of ICRF, mainly on Macs but with some PC versions as well. It is used in a wide variety of ways in our organisation. In some laboratories individuals will run their own databases, while in other cases a group with similar interests will share a common database. Some users put everything into one database while others may set up separate files for different aspects of their work. Often one member of a laboratory or group acts as the gatekeeper, managing the database on behalf of the rest, or more senior staff may expect their secretaries to look after it for them.

Before the advent of *EndNote* a few of the research staff had kept their references in a database on the VAX cluster but this system had never been fully developed and most have now transferred, or are in the process of transferring, to *EndNote*. Their databases have been accumulating for many years and run into thousands of references but *EndNote* appears to handle them quite adequately, provided they have enough disk space on their Macs.

Problems and support

Support for *EndNote Plus* users is shared with the Central Computer Unit. However, we have found that the *EndNote* program itself does not raise many problems, apart from enquiries from those considering buying a copy. Since many of our Mac users rarely log on to the central cluster, many questions relate to the use of VAX programs, such as the E-mail program, the VAX editor or file transfer to the Mac.

The other main area where support has been required is

in importing data via *EndLink*. We have had to adjust our downloading format from time to time as different problems have emerged with non-standard situations. Examples of these have included references with no authors (where we have added a dummy author line) or non-numeric issue numbers. With the introduction of *EndLink 2* in September 1994 it became possible to customise existing filters or create new filters from scratch to support new databases.

Unfortunately, BIDS output does not yet load into *EndNote* without some editing but a program to do this automatically has been provided by David Zeitlyn (E-Mail: zeitlyn@uk.ac.ox.vax), chairman of the BIDS User Group. In general, we have found that *EndNote* has fitted well into working patterns among our research staff and into the services the Library provides.

References

1   DAVIES, Mary. The implementation of *BASIS* at the Imperial Cancer Research Fund. *Program* 25 (3), 1991, 187-206.

Chapter 6 *Papyrus* at the University of Manchester and the CHEST licence
Sarah Davnall, Manchester University Computing Centre

In 1990 the University of Manchester set up a bibliographic software working party to find out what was on the market, examine the most promising packages and recommend one for University use. The self-selected working party consisted of a librarian from each of the two main libraries, a member of the computing service and a member of staff from the Department of Pathological Sciences with an interest in bibliographic matters.

Evaluating packages
Somewhat nonplused to discover that the number of possible packages amounted to nearly fifty, we eventually settled on an evaluation short-list of four: *Pro-Cite* which the librarians had come across although not used; *ideaList* which the computing service knew of as a general text manager; *Library Master* which had been recently announced on the HUMANIST electronic discussion list to which I subscribed and *Papyrus* which our pathologist had heard about in conversation with a colleague who admired its importing capabilities and used it as an interface between CD-ROM sources and *Reference Manager*. *Reference Manager* itself was considered but rejected on the grounds that its suitability was limited to the biomedical fraternity whereas we wanted a package which all disciplines could use. *EndNote* would

also have been a contender but at that time did not have a product for the PC, the supported platform at Manchester, so it too was omitted from the short-list.

The working-party produced an interim report in September 1990 recommending *Papyrus*. Although this product's interface (then at Release 6) left something to be desired, being old-fashioned and without online help, its functionality placed it ahead of all the others. We felt that the range of facilities in *Papyrus* could accommodate usage in all disciplines, while the price would enable us to distribute it widely at minimal cost. We also took the somewhat cynical view that as it was very much cheaper than the others, we would probably be able to afford to invest in a second product later on if *Papyrus* proved unpopular or difficult to support.

We therefore declared our intention of keeping the working party in being in order to repeat our evaluation exercise as new products and new versions of existing products became available. However, our good resolution was never carried out. This was partly due to pressure of work but the main reason was that when it was introduced into the University community *Papyrus* was an instant and resounding success.

Negotiating a site licence for *Papyrus*

Before *Papyrus* could be made available we had to negotiate an appropriate deal with the suppliers. Negotiations were somewhat protracted since it would appear that the concept of the site licence is relatively unknown in the USA and it took some time for Manchester University and Research Software Design to understand each other's requirements. Meanwhile, interest in the working party's conclusions had been expressed by other universities, notably King's College London and Liverpool which also subsequently took out site licences for *Papyrus*. Through Liverpool's connection with the national Database and Free-Text Working Party, the Combined Higher Education Software Team (CHEST) came to hear about *Papyrus* and decided that the software justified investment in a national licensing arrangement.

Manchester was able to make *Papyrus* available in

Chapter 6

about May 1991. King's College London had done so some months earlier but Liverpool was somewhat later. In the end CHEST did not announce its licence until after the release of version 7 of *Papyrus* in May 1992. Whether this was a coincidence or planned it was probably a good thing as it meant that sites did not have to make the transfer from Release 6 to Release 7, the latter having a significantly different (and much improved) interface from that of Release 6 as well as a number of new features which still further enhanced its usefulness.

The CHEST agreement

The CHEST agreement lasts until 30 June 1997 and costs £700 plus VAT per annum for the two current *Papyrus* platforms, PC/DOS and VAX/VMS. Further platforms can be added when available at a charge of £400 plus VAT per annum each. At present, a Mac version is in preparation, for release in 1995. (Although the CHEST agreement mentions a Unix version this is not under development at the time of writing.) Sites taking up the licence receive one copy of the software and documentation which may be reproduced for distribution. Sites may, if they prefer, purchase additional documentation sets from the CHEST Documentation Distribution Service at Manchester University and some sites have found this cost-effective. Manchester also distributes the software which has enabled us to add to the disk set the Manchester-developed library of format definitions for importing references downloaded from such British sources as the Bath Information and Data Service (BIDS). By December 1994 twenty seven universities, one institute of higher education and three research councils have taken site licences under the CHEST agreement.

The site licence permits staff and students of the institution to use *Papyrus* for academic and administrative functions either on campus or elsewhere (e.g. at home). The only restrictions are the standard CHEST ones which primarily prevent commercial exploitation of the software. However, there is no *Papyrus*-related bar (there may be data-related ones!) to the commercial exploitation of any database created by the software and the supplied disk set includes a read-only version of *Papyrus*, the *Retriever*, which users may distribute with their databases provided they do so without additional charge.

Obviously the site licence covers users only while they are members of the holding institution. However, recognising that some users may wish to continue to use their databases after leaving, the CHEST agreement includes a provision whereby sites may sell personal licences to their users which grant the purchaser the same full rights as they would have obtained through a private purchase from Research Software Design. The charge specified by CHEST is £14 plus VAT, plus "a reasonable charge to cover [the institution's] costs for the provision of this additional service".

Using *Papyrus*

Even without the Release 7 improvements, Release 6 was very popular at Manchester. In the year of its existence we issued about 200 licences for use. As licences are issued for machines rather than people, and a significant number of the licences were for public-cluster and departmental/project computers, we would guess that the actual usage of the package was considerably higher. When we made Release 7 available in September 1992, licence issues soared briefly as Release 6 users upgraded and then settled down to about 100 per term. More than 500 licences have been issued. The majority of users are from the biomedical disciplines, as they have always been, this being the area where computerised bibliographic sources have been most developed. However, there are users in all discipline areas, including increasing numbers in the social sciences and humanities.

Funding Papyrus

I don't know how our use of bibliographic software compares with that in other institutions but we are pleased with it. We have not yet reached the dizzy heights of a copy of *Papyrus* for every copy of *WordPerfect* but the level of use is clearly substantial. We believe that this reflects not just the usefulness of the package but also our deliberate policy of encouraging its adoption. We do this by making it available at as small a charge as possible. Release 6, in fact, was distributed to any Manchester University student or member of staff free of charge on a disk-exchange basis. Funding changes meant that this was not feasible for Release 7 but we still do not charge for the licence, merely a cost-recovery amount (totalling £10-12) for the disks and documentation. We are able to do this because the University has the good fortune to possess a software committee with a small budget which decided that bibliographic software was of sufficiently wide academic interest to justify central funding. I hope that this view will continue to prevail despite the devolutionary climate. I feel strongly that we should try to maintain a low-cost policy for *Papyrus* because of its importance to the post-graduate community many of whom suffer significant financial pressure.

Support for users
The other strand of our policy to encourage use of the package was to provide substantial user support, for no manual, however good (and those for *Papyrus* are among the best), can address every detail, even assuming that users will read it. Research Software Design is a small outfit with no external support agents. Help with problems is provided by the company via telephone (unreasonable, in most instances, for Europeans) and electronic mail (fine for those who use it but a significant number do not). It was clear, therefore, that if our users were to obtain sufficient help to enable them to use the software successfully it would have to be provided on-site. This was my task, and at times it has been a full-time one, even though *Papyrus* is supposed to be only one of several database packages in my remit. I provide training through half-day demonstrations, one-day introductory courses and an occasional one-day advanced course, all of which are offered both as part of the regular Manchester Computing Centre course provision and as department-specific courses on request. I also provided some additional documentation for Release 6, although this was less necessary with Release 7, for which Research Software

Design provided a tutorial Workbook. Nevertheless, I am trying to find the time to turn my course notes into a self-teach unit which could be used either by individuals or by those wishing to present courses at other institutions. If I succeed, the unit will be made available through the CHEST Documentation Distribution Service and will be announced on the CHEST *Papyrus* electronic mail discussion list hosted by mailbase (see Appendix 3 for details).

In addition, I receive queries through our usual advisory and help channels. It has been interesting to note how the level and nature of the queries has changed over the period. Initially, and again when version 7 was released, the query level was very high, and consisted mainly of fairly simple enquiries and problems relating to basic usage. Now, except for the start of the Michaelmas term, the queries are fewer but tend to involve more awkward problems. As the level of licence issues indicates a fairly regular addition of new users, it would appear that the simple support effort has devolved to peer groups at the departmental and project level. This is confirmed by the response of quite a number of the users whom I do now help. In the main, they require assistance with getting references from particular sources into *Papyrus* and, after we have been successful, their comments are often along the lines of: "My colleagues all need this as well; I'll make sure I tell them."

Popular features of *Papyrus*
One of the greatest pleasures of supporting *Papyrus* at Manchester has been the number of times I have been told: "It has made my life so much easier". Three features most commonly evoke this comment:

The versatility of the importing capability
Almost any references can be bulk-loaded provided their fields are consistently organised and separated by enough punctuation to indicate where one ends and the next begins.

The Notecards facility
Any number of free-text notes can be linked to a

bibliographic reference in the database and thereafter be searched like keywords.

The ability to interface with a word processor
The ability of the package to interface with a word processor to create in-text citations while a text is being written, subsequently generating from them the matching bibliography. Under DOS, this facility operates in a limited, albeit adequate, way. However, although not a *Windows* product, *Papyrus* will run under *Windows* (or other memory management systems such as the DOS Shell) and will talk to the *Windows* clipboard which permits the full range of *Papyrus* operations including the ability to transfer references suitably formatted for use in footnotes. Users are finding that such capabilities are reducing significantly the labour involved in writing up their research for publication or degree submission.

Conclusions
These features reflect the emphasis implied by the full name of the package: "the *Papyrus* bibliography system". Other software appears to place more emphasis on the management of the bibliographic database but for *Papyrus* this is only one part of the whole bibliography management process. Perhaps for this reason *Papyrus*, at the time of writing, has made less progress than some other products down the networking road. A *Papyrus* database can be installed and accessed over a network but the process is relatively crude and not yet, in my view, entirely successful. This will no doubt change for *Papyrus* is under continuous development. Nevertheless, without denying the importance of a well-structured and well-managed database at the core of the system, *Papyrus* seems, to me, to be more concerned about the use which will be made of it by individuals in pursuit of their personal bibliographic objectives. At Manchester we have many individuals who are very happy with this approach.

Chapter 7 A trial of PC bibliographic database and formatting packages
Eddie Carter, Thornton Research Centre, Shell Research Ltd.

The information scientists at the Thornton Research Centre have found that scientific staff have an increasing need for a tool to handle collections of bibliographic references. Two typical requirements are:
■ as an index to a personal collection of journal articles, reports and other literature
■ as a means of handling a large number of references downloaded from literature searches in order to review a new subject area and/or produce structured annotated bibliographies.

Thornton has a central (mainframe) bibliographic database of its books, reports and other document holdings running under *Basis* software. This is available to all staff and one option would have been to allow users to add personal reference collections to the main database. This option has been rejected in the short term for several reasons. The main database would have become diluted with numerous references outside the Centre's mainstream activities. The inclusion of some journal references in the central database would have led to users expecting comprehensive general literature coverage. Allowing users to have write access to the system would have led to a decrease in data quality, such as non-standard author name formats, thereby leading to poor retrieval. Lastly, there are unresolved copyright implications of putting downloaded references onto a central multiple-access facility.

Numerous database software packages for IBM and IBM-compatible personal computers (PCs) running the DOS operating system are commercially available in the £200-£1,000 price range and have been extensively reported (see bibliography). A project was set up in 1991 to survey the products available, develop some in-house experience and, ultimately, recommend one (or more) packages for use.

Project summary

The project consisted of the following stages:

1. A review of the current journal literature, press releases and trade literature to identify suitable packages for consideration.
2. A survey of user requirements. This was based on interviews with staff who were using (or had expressed interest in using) a PC database package and with staff who had recently carried out extensive literature reviews to see how they had handled the references and if there was a role for PC database software.
3. The selection of packages for evaluation including four that were already available on-site, four which were purchased as a result of the literature review and one (*Personal Librarian*) that was seen at the software suppliers.
4. An evaluation of these package against in-house and published (1 - 3) criteria (Appendix 4).
5. The selection of a short-list of packages for the user trials. These were *Cardbox Plus, ideaList, Pro-Cite* and *Reference Manager*.
6. Sample databases were set up on each package and trials were conducted in the Library as a series of one-to-one demonstrations. Ample time was given for hands-on experience and each person was then asked to complete a simple questionnaire (see Appendix 5) for each package. It was too time-consuming for novices to look at all four packages and so most looked at two or three.

An additional benefit of the trial was the experience gained of a range of PC database packages. As a result we are now better equipped to advise staff on their personal bibliographic information management requirements.

Results and conclusions
The main conclusion, unsurprisingly, is that no package is perfect but some have more strengths than weaknesses.

Reference Manager
The trial identified *Reference Manager* as the clear favourite. It was particularly easy for novice users to get started, to create a database, to input and edit records and to carry out searches. Advanced features include automatic look-up of index terms and duplicate checking at the data input stage. It has a highly structured menu-driven approach, which experienced users may find frustrating, but it copes well with user errors and is robust in operation.

It is fairly straightforward to use the *Capture Module* to import downloaded references from online searches of supported databases on major host systems. Unfortunately, the user cannot develop his own import formats but the software producer has stated a willingness to add new formats to the *Capture Module*. Exporting facilities were found to be awkward and inflexible. The user can develop his own exporting formats (e.g. for input to his own word processor) but this is not a task a novice could undertake. Lastly, at the time of the trial *Reference Manager* had a restrictive range of record types (journal, book, abstract and book chapter) and the user could neither add to nor edit these. It could not, for example, be used to maintain a database of names and addresses of contacts. This limitation has been overcome with the release of Version 6 (for DOS) and *Reference Manager* can now handle thirty four document types.

Pro-Cite
The subjective 'feel' of a product plays a major part in the evaluation of software. Users liked the feel of *Reference*

Manager but, because of the restrictions alluded to above, it may be necessary to offer them alternatives. Although *Pro-Cite* was less popular during the trial it can overcome many of the restrictions found with *Reference Manager*. It would, however, be necessary to purchase a separate package, *Biblio-Links*, for importing downloaded references. Many features of *Pro-Cite* are customisable by the user. One can, for example, design one's own record types (workforms) and import formats in *Biblio-Links*.

Cardbox Plus
This general purpose database package has been in use at Thornton for many years. In view of this expertise it was also considered for the storing of bibliographic data. It is more difficult and time consuming to create a new database with *Cardbox Plus* than it is with *Reference Manager* but field definition is more controllable. The searching facilities are more rudimentary but, for small databases, this is acceptable. *Cardbox Plus* interfaces well with the *Headform* reformatting package for importing downloaded references.

ideaList
This was initially included in the trial but was dropped early on because it was found that users needed a high level of computer intuition and this was off-putting for novices. *ideaList* has, however, many good features including importing and exporting facilities and an ability to handle full text records and may be suitable for the keener computer users. It was the least expensive of the packages evaluated (£225). One unfortunate feature is that when displaying records the user is also able to edit them so that it is easy to alter or erase data without realising.

Packages not included in the trial
Amongst the packages evaluated that were not chosen for the user trials were: *dBase3 plus, FoxPro, Personal Librarian, STN Personal File System* and *Superbase 2*. The reasons for rejecting them were varied but essentially they failed to meet one or more of the criteria of applicability such as

compatibility with existing systems, ease of use with bibliographic data and cost.

dBase3 plus and *FoxPro* are general purpose packages for developing specific database applications. They are not especially aimed at bibliographic applications and it would take some time and effort to develop a bibliographic database. It was decided that *dBase3* and *FoxPro* have a role in the systems development area but are not suitable for the novice user wanting to handle a few references.

Personal Librarian at £995 was the most expensive package considered. It is a full-text database package that uses relevance ranking rather than Boolean searching for information retrieval. Its strength is in searching for clues amongst a mass of text and it is very impressive at this task. It is not, however, designed to handle bibliographic records and its price made it unsuitable for the trial.

Superbase 2 is a general database management system which runs under Microsoft *Windows*. At the time of the trial most scientific staff did not have a PC capable of running *Windows* on their PC and it was decided, after an initial evaluation, to drop *Superbase* from the trial.

STN Personal File System is a bibliographic database package for users of the STN online host. It is not menu-driven but has the same command language as STN. It is easy to import references from any of the databases on STN. Since many other online systems are also used at Thornton a host-specific package would not be suitable.

General problems with the packages
Two irritating features were noted with all the packages. One is the problem of having to jump out of the package to DOS for file management or to run another application and then return to the package. The user generally has to quit the package and then reload it even to browse a file or check a file name. *Pro-Cite* Version 2 includes a menu option to 'visit' DOS. The other general problem is the absence from the menus of all packages of an option for backing up database files, a vital operating procedure. Data representing hours of work can be lost if one forgets to back up files at the

end of a session. It would be advantageous to have menu options for these operations.

The whole arena of bibliographic software is changing rapidly and user expectations are growing. It is difficult to keep abreast of developments as upgrades are continually being brought out for existing products and new products are frequently launched. Our trial was carried with *Reference Manager* version 5.02, *Pro-Cite* version 1.4 and *Cardbox Plus* version 3.5. By the end of the trial, all three had versions with enhanced facilities: *Reference Manager* version 5.05, *Pro-Cite* version 2.0 and *Cardbox Plus* version 4.1. In each case a fee is paid to receive the upgrade.

The reformatting project
It became obvious during the trial that the reformatting of downloaded references for input to personal databases presents a major hurdle. Some packages, such as *Pro-Cite*, require the purchase of a separate reformatting package. Others, including *ideaList* and *Reference Manager*, have an integral Capture Module that can reformat references from many, but not all, of the online databases accessed by Thornton staff. *Cardbox* requires the use of a general reformatting package such as *Headform* to prepare downloaded references for input.

A new project to evaluate reformatting packages to interface with *Reference Manager, Pro-Cite, ideaList* and *Cardbox Plus* was carried out in 1992-3. A survey of currently available packages identified four possibilities:
- *Headform* (4, 5), a general purpose reformatting package developed and marketed by Head Software International
- *RefWriter* (6), a suite of general purpose reformatting programs developed and marketed by Tailored Information Ltd.
- *Biblio-Links* (7, 8, 9) from Personal Bibliographic Software Inc., a reformatting package specifically designed to work with *Pro-Cite*
- *Capture Module*, the optional importing module for *Reference Manager* (10), developed by Research Information Systems Inc. and distributed in the UK by Bilaney Consultants Ltd.

We initially aimed to evaluate each of the reformatting packages with each of our chosen personal bibliographic database packages (i.e. *Reference Manager, ideaList, Pro-Cite* and *Cardbox*) and with data from each of the four online hosts that we regularly use (STN, Dialog, Orbit and ESA/IRS). To do this thoroughly would have involved an excessive amount of work and so we had to be more selective.

We briefly compared *Pro-Cite* and *Biblio-Links* with *Reference Manager* and *Capture* to see if there was any reason to reconsider *Pro-Cite*. We found that *Biblio-Links* reformats references faster than *Capture* and has user customisation facilities that *Capture* lacks but *Capture* was simpler to use and cheaper in price. Since *Reference Manager* was the package favoured by end users in the trial, we decided at this point to abandon any further evaluation of *Pro-Cite* and make *Reference Manager* the site standard package. We encourage the purchase of *Reference Manager* in preference to other packages and support its use. We do not attempt to provide support – or any reformatting service – to users with other bibliographic database packages.

We also decided to concentrate our efforts on reformatting references from the STN and Dialog hosts since they have many of the databases that we use regularly. Although Orbit and ESA/IRS include some useful unique sources, such as *Weldasearch* and *MIRA Abstracts*, we had to accept that we did not have the time to reformat references from every source database and would have to concentrate efforts on our main information sources such as *Chemical Abstracts* and *APILIT*.

The evaluation was, therefore, carried out with data from STN and Dialog, reformatted with *Headform, RefWriter* and *Capture Module* and imported into *Reference Manager*.

Capture Module
We discovered that the *Capture Module* was very good at importing references from the online databases it supported but we could not rely on it for reformatting for two reasons.

Firstly, many of the databases we regularly used were not available as options in the *Capture Module* including, of course, our own in-house databases of corporate information.

Secondly, where a database is available as an option in the *Capture Module*, it may not bring the references into *Reference Manager* in the format that the user wants. For example, the corporate source data is brought into *Reference Manager* inconsistently by the *Capture Module*. From some source databases, the corporate source is put into the keywords field, from others into the abstract field and from others it is not captured at all. This was an important consideration since our users particularly wanted the corporate sources of authors included in their *Reference Manager* databases, especially in the case of patents.

Research Information Systems Inc. have undertaken to make additions to the *Capture Module* for any database/host combination requested by a significant number of users. We have asked for some of our databases, such as *APILIT*, to be added to the *Capture Module* but despite this have decided to write our own reformatting templates to bring over all the data that the users want, and to ensure consistency in the way the data is incorporated into *Reference Manager*. At this point, we had to decide between *Headform* and *RefWriter*.

Headform versus RefWriter
Although *Headform* is simpler to learn than *RefWriter* neither are user friendly and are generally seen as the preserve of the information scientists. The conversion results with *Headform* are good but the successful conversion rate is higher with *RefWriter*. *RefWriter* has many more conversion facilities than *Headform*, although *Headform* does have some capabilities that *RefWriter* does not possess. *RefWriter* was found to be much faster than *Headform* at reformatting large files with several hundred references.

In addition to references from external databases, we also wanted to be able to reformat references from some of our in-house databases. *Headform* was incapable of handling references from one database, an old system which has inconsistent data structures and field tags with spaces or punctuation as part of the tag, whilst *RefWriter* could cope with a reasonable degree of accuracy.

RefWriter has been adopted as the software for reformatting data for input to *Reference Manager*.

General problems with reformatting
Which ever reformatting package is chosen there are many problems and pitfalls to avoid in order to get clean records from a source database into the target database. Much time and effort can be expended in a frustrating search for ways around these problems. Lack of a standard format for storing references in bibliographic databases has been commented on in the literature (11). Some of the main problems we discovered during the evaluation are:

Inconsistency in source records
If the tags or delimiter to differentiate between sub fields, fields and records are inconsistent in the source database, the reformatting package will not be able to transcribe the data correctly

Errors within source records
Common examples are the omission of delimiters between sub fields and the placing of information in the reference field in the wrong order. Again the reformatting software cannot transcribe the data correctly.

Field tags
Field tags that do not start in the first column, or contain spaces or punctuation, or are longer than 10 characters, cannot be handled by some reformatting packages.

Author's names
There is no standard for the format of names and sometimes within one database, names may be formatted differently.

Records to different media types
The personal bibliographic database needs to know the media type of a record in order to ascribe the correct fields. For example a conference paper requires a conference title, editor and publisher whereas a journal paper requires a journal

name and volume. Patent references are handled as if they were journal papers with, for example, US patent as the journal name and the patent number as the volume number.

Indentation within source records
Many reformatting programs cannot cope if the field tag does not begin in the first column. Only *RefWriter* can handle this situation without initial text editing, e.g. to remove character spaces before the field tag.

Extraneous information
Text such as page headers that is not part of the records can disrupt the reformatting process.

The source field
Extracting data such as volume number, page numbers and publication dates from a 'catch all' source field is a particular problem.

Delimited formats
These were found hard to reformat where there were no line breaks within records. Some reformatting software cannot handle long lines without truncating and losing data.

File size
The larger the source file, the more likely it is that the reformatting software will make a mistake. It is preferable to reformat a series of small files. Errors are then easier to locate and correct.

Enhancements to *Reference Manager*
Despite having to make the case for purchasing the software and paying for it from their departmental budgets there has been a slow but steady uptake of *Reference Manager* amongst end users at Thornton.

WinRM
The Microsoft *Windows* version of *Reference Manager* (version 5.51, also known as *WinRM*) launched in May 1993

(12, 13) has considerable advantages over the DOS version including pull-down menus, full compatibility with *Word for Windows* for producing bibliographies and compatibility with all the other facilities of *Windows*. At that time, *WinRM* was the only personal bibliographic database that was fully compatible with Microsoft *Windows*, and we had no hesitation in recommending those users who had a 486 Windows PC to purchase *WinRM* in preference to the DOS version (*Reference Manager* version 5.06). An upgrade version is also available.

Reference Manager Network Edition
At the end of 1994 RIS announced the *Reference Manager Network Edition* for PC based networks supporting DOS or Windows and for *Windows for Workgroups* peer to peer networks. The licence fee is based on the number of databases which can be created.

Delivery of search results
The feedback we have had from users so far is that they find *Reference Manager* a very useful tool for personal information management. Two common types of usage are worthy of noting here:
- as a database to index a personal collection of journal articles, reports, company notes and other documents. The facility to assign accession numbers to documents based on one's own filing categories is particularly useful.
- maintaining a database of all documents known to be of interest in a particular subject area, e.g for a project.

The references may be keyed in manually (which gives the option for including personal notes and comments on a reference) or may be a selection of references downloaded from both in-house and external databases.

Users have the option of receiving their literature search results in RIS format (a simple format for importing or exporting data to or from *Reference Manager*) in addition to the conventional options of print-on-paper or as an ASCII file. References are reformatted with a suite of customised templates that we have written for our main source databases using *RefWriter*.

Results are delivered on diskette and references can be easily imported into *Reference Manager* in one of two ways: by a bulk load of all references or by individual selection with the option of editing references before importing them into the *Reference Manager* database.

Delivery of SDI results in RIS format is our next goal. In view of the time taken reformatting searches we have only offered this service to a few selected users at present. Further work is in progress.

References

1   SIEVERTS, E. G. et al., *Microcomputer applications for online and local information systems: a test and comparison of 30 packages*. Leiden: VOGEN, 1987

2   SIEVERTS, E. G. et al., Software for information storage and retrieval tested, evaluated and compared (in four parts). Part 1, *Electronic Library* 9 (3), 1991, 145-154; Part 2, 9 (6), 1991, 301-316; Part 3, 10 (1), 1992, 5-18; Part 4, 10 (4), 1992, 195-207.

3   NIEUWENHUYSEN, P. Criteria for the evaluation of text storage and retrieval software. *Electronic Library* 6 3) 1988, 160-166.

4   TONSING, R.E. Downloading and reformatting external records for researchers' personal databases. *Program* 25 (4), October 1991, 303-317.

5   SIEVERTS, E.G. Software for the conversion of downloaded data: criteria for comparison and assessment. In: *Online Information 89. Proceedings of the 13th IOLIM, London, 12-14 December 1989*, pp. 59-70. Oxford: Learned Information, 1989.

6   ANON. *RefWriter*: a new data conversion package. *Library Micromation News* 32 (June), 1991, 12-14.

7   ROSENBERG, V. *Pro-Search, Biblio-Links* and *Pro-Cite*: software to gather and manage scientific and technical information. *Biotechniques* 10, 1991, 796-797.

8   HANSON, T.A. The Electronic Current Awareness Service and the use of *Pro-Cite* at Portsmouth Polytechnic. In: *Online Information 90. Proceedings of the 14th IOLIM, London, 11-13 December 1990*, edited by D.I. Raitt, pp. 277-287. Oxford: Learned Information (Europe) Ltd., 1990.

9   HANSON, T.A. Pro-Cite and *Biblio-Links. Library Micromation News* 26 (December), 1989, 10-12.

10 JONES, R.G. Personal computer software for handling references from CD-ROM and mainframe sources for scientific and medical reports. *BMJ.* 307, 1993, 180-184.

11 POYNDER, R. Software producers seek common standard for storing records. *Information World Review* 19 (83), 1993, 19.

12 RABINOWITZ, R. *Reference Manager* for DOS; *Reference Manager*, Professional Edition for Windows. (Software Review of Version 5.06 for DOS and version 5.5 for Windows from Research Information Systems Inc., two of six evaluations of bibliography programs in 'Point of Reference'). *PC Magazine* 12 (October), 1993, 271-278.

13 SIMON, B. Bibliography builders. (Software Review of Research Information Systems' *Reference Manager* 5.5 for Windows, one of eight scientific software evaluations in 'The Essential Scientific Toolkit'). *Windows Sources* 1 (September), 1993, 324.

Chapter 7

Acknowledgements
The author acknowledges the contributions of Jill Gilliland, Karen Moorhouse and Clare Cotter, sandwich students from Loughborough University of Technology, 1991-4, in carrying out this work.

Chapter 8 Electrocopying from databases
David Slee, Centre for Legal Studies, University of Hertfordshire

The lawyer is often called upon to warn of the dangers involved in whatever activities some other profession is undertaking. Although it is indeed appropriate to indulge in cautionary advice when the activity concerned is the downloading of records from commercially produced bibliographic databases for storage and manipulation using bibliographic software, I would like also to play a more constructive role. The question of intellectual property rights is one area of the law where rights and obligations are subject to free negotiation. This means either that rights can be surrendered, against a payment of a fee, or that rights can be clearly defined or even amplified to a degree not possible within the framework of the basic legislation.

Whichever choice is made by the rights holder the mechanism which allows for this is the law of contract. It would, as a consequence, be unrealistic to talk about the one without reference to the other.

In this paper I would like firstly to discuss the nature of databases and the sources of copyright or other forms of protection which they may attract and, secondly, I will comment on the role of contract law within this schema (1). A third purpose of the paper is to look at the EC Draft Directive (2) on the protection of databases which in some respects transcends both the previous areas.

Chapter 8

The proposed EC legislation in some ways confirms existing rules concerning databases whilst at the same time drawing the rules into new and uncharted waters. If the proposal is to become legislation perhaps it is best to approach the principal aims of the paper through the directive.

The Directive's definition of a database
A database is defined by the directive as:

> "... a collection of works or materials arranged, stored or accessed by electronic means, and electronic materials necessary for the operation of the database such as its thesaurus, index or system for presenting information; it shall not be taken to apply to any computer program used in the making or operation of the database."

The exclusion of the program is to be expected as the EC has already issued a directive on the legal protection of computer programs (3).
The definition recognises that there are different ways in which copyright rules can impact upon a database.

Content of the database
The first and most obvious way is that a database, whether electronic or not, is a collection of 'items'. These items might themselves be copyright works in their own right. They may have been created by the same person who created the database or by somebody else as the case may be. If the latter is the case then the traditional forms of copyright still prevail to protect the right holder in the original 'item' so that the database author must have, by exemption (notably the fair dealing provisions) or by permission, the right to include the works in the content of the database. This is reinforced by the directive which states, in Article 4:

> "The incorporation into a database of other works or materials remains subject to copyright or other rights acquired or obligations incurred therein."

If the 'items' constituting the content were created by the database author then such an individual will enjoy dual protection. This is the traditional form of copyright. However, under the terms of the draft EC directive this traditional form is now subject to express exemptions, namely Article 4 which states:

> "The incorporation into a database of bibliographical material or brief abstracts, quotations or summaries which do not substitute for the original works themselves, shall not require the authorisation of the right holders in those works."

One must be clear that this is a protection for the database author as against the right holder in the copyright items incorporated into the database. It is not intended as a protection for the unauthorised database user against the rights of the database author (4).

However an even greater change is heralded. The directive includes another type of right which relates to the contents of the database and runs alongside the traditional copyright form of protection. The new right is introduced by Article 2 and seeks to prevent what is termed 'unfair extraction'. It is not generically a right of copyright, it stems rather from the idea of unfair competition. The new right does not seek to interfere with the traditional copyright either in terms of the database as a collection) or the 'items' which it contains. Article 2 states:

> "A database shall be protected by copyright if it is original in the sense that it is a collection of works or material which, by reason of their selection or arrangement, constitutes the author's own intellectual creation. No other criteria shall be applied to determine the eligibility of a database for this protection."

> "The copyright protection of a database given by this directive shall not extend to the works or materials contained therein irrespective of whether or not they are

themselves protected by copyright; the protection of a database shall be without prejudice to any rights subsisting in those works or materials themselves."

In effect the article is making the assumption that normal copyright already applies in the content. If that is not the case the article is certainly not going to extend copyright to cover it. What it provides instead is a:

"...right for the maker of a database to prevent the unauthorised extraction or utilisation from that database of its contents, in whole or in substantial part, for commercial purposes ... (the right) shall apply irrespective of the eligibility of that database for protection under copyright."

To make the fact that the right is non-aligned with copyright that much clearer the article concludes by saying:

"It (the right) shall not apply to the contents of a database where these works are already protected by copyright or neighbouring rights."

The period of protection offered shall (Article 9) "... run as of the date of creation of the database and shall expire at the end of a period of ten years from the date when the database is first lawfully made available to the public..."

To avoid any unnecessary bloodshed in the courtroom as to the exact date on which the database was "made available" the provisions deem this to have occurred on 1 January in the given year.

Limitations on the new right
The new right is subject to three important limitations.

1   Where a person has lawfully acquired the right to use a database it is, and must be, possible for that person to reproduce small extracts by way of quotation or reference. This reasonable requirement is provided for in two ways, although in each case it must be stressed that the provision only applies to an extraction or utilisation of an "insubstantial part" of the work (as is usual this is tested qualitatively, not quantitatively). Firstly, if the intention is use for commercial purposes there must be an acknowledgement of source. Secondly, if for personal and private use no acknowledgement is necessary.

One can see problems here for academics who carry out personal research, which is, at a later date, published. It is worth repeating that contract is the key.

2   The ten year period of protection cannot be artificially extended by making insubstantial changes to the database. Databases are not, unlike Peter Pan, copyrights which don't grow up.

3   The third limitation is quite complex. If the works or materials contained in a database, which is made publicly available, are such that they cannot be obtained from any other source, then, extraction and utilisation of them, for commercial purposes is subject to a compulsory licence. The rule also applies to public bodies charged with assembling or disclosing information, provided that they make such information available to the public. This means that criminal records held by the police are not subject to licence as they do not make these available to the public. On the other hand publicly available records of, for example, a local authority might be.

The database as a collection

Collections of literary or artistic works whether electronic or not have traditionally been given copyright protection on the basis that the selection or arrangement of the materials which form the content of the collection necessitates an expenditure of skill, labour and capital such as to justify that protection. Under the new proposals for electronic databases these criteria remain, as already mentioned, in Article 2:

> "A database shall be protected by copyright if it is original in the sense that it is a collection of works or material

which, by reason of their selection or arrangement, constitutes the author's own intellectual creation. No other criteria shall be applied to determine the eligibility of a database for this protection."

Arguably, if no such process can be identified then no copyright protection should be given. This would be the case for example with an alphabetical list of all telephone subscribers, as opposed to a list selected on the basis of profession, locality, etc. The consequence of this is that a collection of information may achieve copyright protection neither in terms of the 'items' which form the database (they might simply be a complete list of names) nor in the collection (they are arranged alphabetically). It was for this reason that the draft directive introduced the right, outlined above, against unfair extraction.

How then is a database author to know whether copyright, based on the collection, or only the lesser right of protection against unfair extraction is available? It is not possible currently to give a clear answer. Even the Commission, when introducing the draft directive, said:

"This directive cannot determine the minimum number of items to be selected or arranged in order to qualify for copyright protection as a collection."

What can be said is that the answer lies in the level of originality. In the UK the level of selection and arrangement necessary to allow protection has traditionally been very low. The courts have operated on the basis that if something is worth taking it is prima facie worth protecting, although clearly the less original or selective the work (in this case the database) the higher degree of similarity required between the original and the copy to establish infringement. This, in the context of electronic downloading, is a difficult concept for what is being transferred is an exact copy of the content. However, assuming for the moment that the appropriate level of originality can be proved then one problem can be regarded as solved, but others remain.

Digitised versus material form
The fact that computerised databases allow for the storage of collections from many different sources in a digitised, rather than material, form is of no real relevance, subject to two reservations.

Firstly, the computerised database has the capacity to store not only large amounts but also a wide variety of information in digitised form. This information might attract a variety of different types of copyright ranging from literary, dramatic and musical works on the one hand to artistic works on the other (one need only look at multi-media systems to exemplify the range of potential inputs). As a result the database author needs to take care in ensuring that the creation of the database does not infringe those copyrights (see the comments on content above). The old definition of copying, which needed "material form" has been replaced by s17(2) of the Copyright Designs and Patents Act 1988 (CDPA) which states: "Copying ... includes storing the work in any medium by electronic means."

It is also perhaps worth noting that the word "translation" within s21 of CDPA which deals with "making of an adaptation" is defined as: "...converted into or out of computer language." Although admittedly s21(4) is referring to a computer program. Equally, according to s21(1) of the same act: "... an adaptation is made when it (the work) is recorded, in writing, or otherwise." Writing, according to s178: "... includes any form of notation or code."

Secondly, as the database gets wider and the consequent user selection gets more sophisticated the balance of skill between the database owner and the user becomes blurred, even if the user is guided through the search procedures to the database contents by the underlying software. In addition to the "unfair extraction" rights noted earlier the exclusive rights of the database author based on the selection and arrangement copyright allow the prohibition of any reproduction, translation, adaptation or other alteration which would result in these acts being done to a sufficiently large proportion of the database to constitute a "substantial taking" or infringement of the selection or arrangement. This would be equally true if that substantial taking was further distributed, communicated or displayed to the public. However, if what was taken was insubstantial, was isolated from the remainder of the database it would be difficult for the database author as opposed to the content copyright owner to claim an infringement.

Defining infringement of the database author's rights
What then constitutes an infringement of the database author's rights? Article 5 of the draft directive gives the database author the exclusive right to do or authorise the following:
- the temporary or permanent reproduction of the database by any means and in any form, in whole or in part
- the translation, adaptation, arrangement and any other alteration of the database
- the reproduction of the results of either of the above
- any form of distribution to the public, including rental (this is particularly important as the database market on CD-ROM grows, as against the online services)
- any communication, display or performance of the database to the public.

As a control of these limitations Article 6 allows derogation to the extent necessary to allow the user to actually use the database, namely: the lawful user of a database may perform any of the acts listed in Article 5 which is necessary in order to use that database *in the manner determined by the contractual arrangement with the rightholder.*

Note again the variation of rights by contract. Before leaving the issue of infringement one other aspect is important in relation to databases, authorising an infringement. Section 12(2) CDPA states:

> "Copyright in a work is infringed by a person who without the licence of the copyright owner does, or authorises another to do so, any of the acts restricted by the copyright."

Such an authorisation is clearly of relevance to intermediaries within an information system as well as those who provide the means to infringe. In this context the two cases involving Amstrad (5) are useful. Both cases centred around the manufacture by Amstrad of a twin deck tape machine, sales of which were advertised phrases such as: "You can even make a copy of your favourite cassettes."

The court took note of the fact that not only would most consumers use the machines for the purposes of infringing copyright but also that Amstrad knew this to be the case. However, Amstrad was ultimately found not to have authorised such infringements as they had, in a written notice, warned consumers of the need to respect copyright laws. Amstrad even admitted to the court that they knew that very few consumers either read or acted upon the notice. Yet the fact that the notice had been issued excused Amstrad from liability. If nothing else the case illustrates the value of making matters clear, in a contract.

Electrocopying

Where does all of this leave the role of electrocopying from on-line or CD-ROM databases and where does it leave those who promote the process? In strict terms the situation is fraught with difficulty. In effect, the use of programs to capture and translate databases (or selections of databases) into common codings so as to allow a reformatting or merging of the down-loaded records is potentially an infringement of at least the database author's copyright in the collection and also potentially the copyright of the content owner who may or may not be the same person as the database author. It is also a potential infringement of the "unfair extraction" provisions. The user may be the most likely person to infringe but one must not lose sight of the potential of infringement by authorisation.

The saving grace is contract

It is not possible here to examine all the ramifications of the contractual relationship. However, some general comments can be made about the ability of contracts to deal with situations.

Chapter 8

1. Contracts can give a business party who uses them effectively the control of a relationship or set of relationships. This is of particular importance to those acting as intermediaries where loose control can place them in a position which is attacked from both sides; the user and the rights holder. The control is not, however, a total control in that there are statutes covering contractual mechanisms such as implied terms, exclusion clauses and the like.
2. Contracts can allow for the definition of rights and duties in a way which is simply not possible through the legislation. Indeed much of the criticism levelled at UK copyright legislation has been in terms of the lack of precision (6). The contract can surmount this difficulty.
3. Contracts can make statements relevant to third parties. The use of such a statement by Amstrad perhaps made all the difference to the decision on their liability.

The need for contract is not simply a need for the user to protect himself. It must be regarded by the database owners as a marketing opportunity. Contracts are there not just to keep the parties at arm's length, they are mechanisms for defining and stratifying the market. Some users will be content with very limited access, perhaps with a computer printout at the end of the process. Others will want the facility to download the records to disk. The latter group should not be prevented simply because the lack of clarity in either the EC directive or the UK legislation. The rules of copyright simply provide the starting point for contractual negotiation. The well-drafted, sectionalised/customised/stratified contract will solve most, if not all, problems. As for the directive, whilst it is not law yet the environment seems set for it to be so, despite industry reservations. What can at least be said for the draft directive is that to a great extent it defines the status quo and still allows the necessary variation by contract to take place. As to the more novel aspects ... time will tell.

Notes and references

1. The major contractual issues are dealt with in: SLEE, D. Liability for information provision. *Law Librarian*, 23 (3) 1992, 155-160.

2. COMMISSION OF THE EUROPEAN COMMUNITIES. *Proposal for a Council Directive on the legal protection of databases.* COM(92) 24 FINAL. The Commission, 1992.

3. COMMISSION OF THE EUROPEAN COMMUNITIES. Proposal for a Council Directive on the legal protection of computer programs. *Official Journal of the EC*. L122, 17/5/91, 42-46.

4. It must be remembered too that this relaxation would only apply to copyright. Also under new EC proposals such information may now be classified as personal data and be subject to data protection requirements. Of the present draft directive Article 12 clearly indicates that the directive's provisions are "without prejudice to copyright or any other right subsisting including confidentiality, data protection and privacy."

5. AMSTRAD CONSUMER ELECTRONICS PLC. V. THE BRITISH PHONOGRAPH INDUSTRY LTD. [1986] FSR 159; CBS Songs Ltd. v. Amstrad Consumer Electronics plc [1987] 3 All ER 151

6. SLEE, D. and HOBSON, J.B. Transactional and semantic indeterminacy in statutory modelling. *Law, Computers and Artificial Intelligence* 1 (2) 1992, 203-218.

Chapter 9 Staying within the law
Charles Oppenheim, Professor of Information Science, University of Strathclyde

Introduction
Copyright protects the labour, skill and judgement of someone – author, artist or some other creator – expended in the creation of an original piece of work whether it is a book, a piece of music, a painting, a photograph or whatever. Different countries in the world apply different tests in order for copyright to be enjoyed; in countries with the UK tradition of law the emphasis is on 'the sweat of the brow' – in other words, sheer hard work is rewarded even if what is created is nothing terribly profound (although it must still be *new*). In countries with a Continental European tradition of law the emphasis is on the intellectual creativity and mere hard work is not enough. The owner of the copyright has the right to prevent anyone else from reproducing, selling, hiring out, copying in any form, performing in public, broadcasting on radio or TV, destroying or amending the copyright work. These acts are the so-called *restricted acts*.

Virtually anything that is written, printed or recorded in some other way can be the subject of such copyright protection. The owner's copyright rights, preventing others from doing certain acts, are limited in various ways. The most significant limitations are by time – typically, copyright in a literary work lasts for fifty years beyond the author's death and they are limited by amounts being copied – as we will see, third parties are permitted to copy small portions of a literary work without approval.

The legal term for material, typically text and numbers, that is held in databases and can be downloaded and stored, is 'Literary Work'. Don't be misled by the term 'Literary' there is no implication that this is quality literature. Under the Act, a piece in the *Sunday Sport* is just as much a literary work as a set of records from *Chemical Abstracts* and equally worthy of protection. You should note that there is no copyright in a fact, or indeed in a book title, basic bibliographic data (such as an abstract number, or OPAC record) or similar items.

There is a special type of literary work called 'compilations'. This is a collection of works, each of which may or may not be subject to individual copyright – a good example is a bibliography, a set of catalogue records or a database comprising a set of records whether full text or abstracts.

The collection or compilation has in many countries of the world with a 'sweat of the brow' tradition – including the UK – its own copyright because skill and effort was expended making the collection.

Typically, copyright in literary works lasts for fifty years from the end of the calendar year when the author died. If the literary work is an anonymous work or it is not known when the author died, it lasts for fifty years from the end of the year when the work was first published – in other words, when multiple copies were first issued to the public. This would normally apply in the case of the types of material that are downloaded.

Handling full text

So, here we have a literary work in machine readable form. Copyright law says no-one except the owner may copy it – and copying includes downloading data from it. Can you download the data? The answer is: you can only do so if one of two circumstances apply. The first is that your contract permits you to do it (I will discuss contracts later on in this chapter), the second is that there are a number of important exceptions to the rule about not being able to copy. I want to look at the most important of these exceptions – fair dealing. Curiously for such an important and universal concept, it is not defined in law at all. Fair dealing basically means that an individual may make a copy of not too substantial a part of a literary work as long as the copying does not damage the legitimate interests of the copyright owner and as long as it is for one of the purposes specified in the local legislation. The UK law permits fair dealing for: research, private study, criticism and book reviewing, and reporting current events. I want to look at just one of these in detail – fair dealing for the purposes of research or private study.

My definition of 'fair dealing' begs a lot of questions. For example, what is deemed 'substantial'? UK law offers no guidelines, and there are very few court decisions to rely on, but generally people seem to regard anything less than 10 per cent of the original length as being acceptable.

Anything more and it could well be deemed 'substantial' but it all depends on the particular circumstances. For example, the final line of a detective story, where the detective announces to the people gathered round who did the murder and how, may not be 'substantial' in terms of length but reproduction (say in a book review) may well spoil sales for the copyright owner and would therefore certainly be considered 'substantial'. Indeed, one useful approach is to consider whether the material taken for fair dealing would be *considered an adequate substitute for the original*, meaning a person reading the extract feels he no longer needs to see the original. If that is the case, then it is likely this is indeed 'substantial' and is not 'fair dealing' but is infringement.

What about 'research or private study'? The term is fairly self explanatory although it is worth stressing that private study is by no means just linked to formal courses of study but for any private purpose, and that 'research' can be academic research, industrial research or any other sort, whether for profit or not. UK law states that the person wanting the copy should make the copy him or herself or someone else may be authorised to make the copy on his or her behalf. This would certainly apply to information officers making copies on behalf of their patrons. Fair dealing applies to books, journal articles and databases equally.

The other possible major applications of fair dealing are for criticism or review or for reporting current events. The former is self evident – you can quote from a book, etc. in the course of a review; the latter permits someone, say, to create a news clippings service although this is *not* the same as an SDI service using journal articles.

Information officers, typically, can make copies from electronic full text, subject to the fair dealing provisions, on behalf of their patrons. Typically, they are, *if requested to do so*, permitted to make single copies of individual articles in a journal for their patrons. The law may not make clear what is or is not an 'article', so it is best to use common sense and, for example, to regard an editorial as an article, an individual article as an article obviously, a letter to the editor as an article and so on. The library may also make copies of a reasonable proportion of any book or monograph upon request to the patron – 'reasonable' being undefined but 10 per cent maximum would be a good working rule. These rules would apply equally to creating downloaded copies for third parties. You should treat the electronic data as if it were printed and follow the same ground rules as you would for printed materials. In other words, you may only make the copies on receipt of a suitable form, signed by the individual declaring he or she wants the item for the purposes of research or private study and confirming that a copy has not previously been supplied to him. The user is required to make a payment which covers the cost of making the copy plus any overheads associated with the copying facility. *The library cannot take the initiative* and send the individual a downloaded item or items in the confident anticipation that he or she will be interested in it. There is no question that electronic bulletins containing, say, the contents pages of new journals, are illegal unless individually requested every time by the patron.

Handling other databases
What is the impact of copyright on database producers,

Chapter 9

online hosts and those people who use online hosts and CD-ROMs to retrieve information? The first thing to note is that UK copyright law is very ambiguous and vague in this field. This is because the concept of a 'database' is not understood by legislators; some people claim the ambiguity is deliberate to allow for many years of technological advance before our Act need be amended; it is my view that it reflects the lack of knowledge by legislators about such matters. However, it is clear that most electronic databases, whether comprising words or numbers, will be considered as 'compilations', whilst individual records within the database may or may not be subject to copyright, depending on whether they are simple facts (no copyright) or a genuine text such as abstracts.

It is clear, therefore, that under UK law, a database of machine readable records, is likely to be regarded as a 'literary work' within the meaning of the Act. This will certainly apply to floppy disc databases, CD-ROM databases and the like. What about online databases? Some commentators believe that online databases are also covered by Section 7 of the Act as 'cable programmes'. In theory, this could have significant ramifications, as concepts such as 'fair dealing' have no application to 'cable programmes'. In fact, copyright barristers say that although in theory the wording of the Act could lend itself to this interpretation, in practice no British court of law would be likely to adopt that position. The majority view is that online databases, too, are simply literary works, but readers should be aware that there is genuine ambiguity and disagreement on the matter.

Assuming databases are deemed to be compilations within the broad heading of 'literary works', librarians and information scientists in theory may make copies of parts of such literary works for their clients in just the same way that they may make photocopies of full text items. The same ground rules of 'fair dealing', of not taking more than a reasonable portion of the entire work apply. On the other hand, in many cases (such as an abstracts service), each individual record is *also* subject to copyright, so you should not interpret this to mean you can download a number of abstracts records and as you would, then, be infringing the

copyright of the individual abstracts. In the case of databases where the individual items do not enjoy copyright in their own right, such as a library catalogue, you could in theory download and store a 'reasonable' proportion under the fair dealing provisions without permission.
In practice, of course, the question of fair dealing is irrelevant as what clients may or may not do with output from online databases is controlled by the contract with the host operator.
So, users must abide by the terms of the contract, specifically those regarding downloading and re-dissemination of the data. These contractual terms take precedence over any copyright law terms. If a client willingly signs a contract, and assuming the clauses are not invalid in law because they are too one-sided or are unreasonable, then he must abide by the contract.

Recent EC initiatives on copyright
During the first half of 1992 the Commission published two Draft Directives of direct relevance. The first proposes that copyright on literary works to be extended from fifty years to seventy years. German copyright law already has seventy years but the vast majority of countries in the world have adopted fifty years. The practical significance of this proposed change is small. The material in most databases are out of date by the time they are twenty five years old, let alone fifty or seventy years old.

The EC Draft Directive on Database Copyright – Introduction
The Draft Directive for the Copyright Protection of Databases is, of course, far more germane to the question of electronic copyright. I will examine only the most relevant Articles in this Chapter:
The Directive's Article 1 defines a 'database' as:

> " ...a collection of works or materials arranged, stored and accessed by electronic means, and the electronic materials necessary for the operation of the database such as its thesaurus, index or system for obtaining or presenting

information; it shall not be taken to apply to any computer program using in the making or the operation of the database."

This definition clearly covers databases on floppy disc, real time financial information, newswires and feeds, CD-ROMs, OPAC collections, videotext, audiotext and of course online. The definition also covers thesauri and systems for presenting the information, such as keywording, use of fields, etc.

Article 2, Section 1 states: "... Member States shall protect databases by copyright as collections within the meaning .... of Literary ... Works". The same Article states that a database can only be protected by copyright as a literary work if it is:

"... original in the sense that it is a collection of works or materials which, by reason of their selection or their arrangement, constitutes the author's own original intellectual creation. No other criterion shall be applied ..."

So, originality is the sole criterion. By adopting such a standard, the Commission has taken a half-way house position between the Anglo-American approach of 'sweat of the brow, but new' and the Continental European approach of higher intellectual creativity. Note, too, that the originality must be in the selection or arrangement.

This Article also makes it clear that individual items within a database may or may not enjoy their own copyright protection. Thus, a database can be protected by copyright even though none of the contents is protected by copyright. An example of an individual item that does enjoy its own copyright protection is a recent abstract produced by, say, *Chemical Abstracts or Reuter Textline.*

An example of an individual item that does not enjoy its own copyright would be an entry in a telephone directory or a share price as those sorts of items are facts, and facts do not enjoy copyright.

Another example of an item that does not enjoy

copyright is a *Chemical Abstracts* abstract which is more than fifty years old. So, the Directive makes it clear that if you put together a database made up of items which are owned by someone else, that someone else still owns the copyright to the individual items and you must, therefore get formal permission to use that material but it is you who owns the copyright to the collection as a collection, because it is you who put skill and effort into building it up.

Article 4 states that:

"The incorporation into a database of bibliographic material or brief abstracts, quotations or summaries which do not substitute for the original works themselves shall not require the authorisation of the rights holder of those works."

So it is clear you can write your own abstracts for your database without infringing the copyright of the original document – as long as the abstracts do not act as substitutes!

Article 5 states that the owner can prevent third parties from doing 'restricted acts' such as: the reproduction of all or part of the database either temporarily (for example by downloading) or permanently; the translation, adaptation or arrangement of the database, or the publication of results of such acts; or the distribution or the display to the public of the database.

There are certain limitations to these database owner's rights. These are listed in Articles 6 and 7 and include the right of a lawful user to do things permitted by a contract he or she has the database producer. In the unlikely event of no formal contract, the lawful user can do such acts as are necessary to gain access to the database. In addition, as you might expect, fair dealing for the purposes of research and private study is permitted if it is permitted in the local national law.

Article 9 of the Draft states that the term of protection for databases shall be the same as for literary works. As noted earlier, the Commission is proposing to extend the period of copyright from fifty years to seventy years.

The same Article in the Draft Directive introduces a new *sui generis* protection for databases whose individual contents do not merit copyright protection. It states that for such compilations, the *sui generis* right to prevent unfair extraction shall last for fifteen years from the date that the database was first lawfully offered to the public. The new *sui generis* right would apply to listings such as telephone directories and share price listings, etc. In such cases, the protection is the untested and unknown one of 'unfair extraction' and lasts fifteen years.

Finally, this Article states that:

> "Insubstantial changes to the contents of a database shall not extend the original period of protection of that database by the right to prevent unfair extraction."

Similar wording appears elsewhere regarding databases whose individual contents are protected by copyright. Unfortunately, no definition of 'insubstantial' is supplied. The length of protection for a database which is continually being added to, a few hundreds records per week say, would, under this Directive last just fifty/seventy years (if individual items are subject to copyright) or fifteen years (if individual items are not subject to copyright) from the date the database was first offered to the public.

Thus an old database, such as *Chemical Abstracts* would date its copyright from the first date it was offered to the public in electronic form (early 1960s?) and the entire *Chemical Abstracts* database, even the most recent items, would cease to protected by copyright in the 2030s; other database comprising non-copyright material, such as say *Tradstat* or *Datastream* would, under the terms of this Directive, have no "right to prevent unfair extraction" immediately, as more than fifteen years have passed since they were first offered to the public in electronic form. Some experts have argued that the expansion of a database to cover a new source would be a 'substantial' change and therefore would extend the database's life, perhaps indefinitely if new sources were regularly added. The

Commission officials seem to think such a change would not be a 'substantial' change. Time will tell when somewhere a court makes a ruling on the subject!

Conclusions on the EC Draft Directive
To conclude on this Draft Directive: I welcome the clear definition of databases and the clear statement that databases will be protected under copyright as literary works. I am, however, concerned about the Commission's approach to the updating of databases. My own view is that each added item or items should start their own clock ticking. Therefore a database with a long backfile, say more than fifty years old, will have some (older) records which are out of copyright, some which are about to go out of copyright and many records still in copyright. Although not so easy to police in terms of infringement, it seems the fairest approach.

Finally, I am concerned about the *sui generis* right for certain types of databases, which do not deserve full copyright protection, for the following reasons:

1 The term 'unfair extraction', although defined in the Draft Directive, has no track record in law and is, therefore, uncertain for database producers, users and Courts to interpret.
2 The period of fifteen years' protection seems inadequate considering the fifty (or even seventy) years other databases whose individual records are copyrightable enjoy. Similar expenditure of time, effort and money may go into the creation of both types of database.
3 It is a mistake to try to distinguish electronic and print publications in this way, especially as these days print publications are frequently produced from electronic equivalents. A printed telephone directory will end up with fifty (or seventy) years' full copyright protection – and only fifteen years' weaker protection in electronic form even though the chances are the print form was created from the electronic form.

However, we should keep the question in proportion. Most of the databases we use are either those which have individual items which are copyright and/or where skill has been used in collecting and selecting items in them and, therefore, full copyright protection will apply to them.

Conclusions

UK law on downloading currently contains a number of ambiguities, particularly because 'databases' are not defined and because the status of online databases is ambiguous. The proposed EC Draft Directive – which is, at the time of writing (November1994), currently going through its legislative process and may emerge unscathed, with major changes or may be dropped altogether – sweeps away some of these ambiguities (for example, the Commission has made it clear that the Directive will replace UK legislation and not sit 'side by side' with it and online databases will be clearly 'literary works' in law), but, unfortunately, at the same time will introduce further problems, particularly in creating its new *sui generis* right for those databases not comprising their own copyright items.

The Draft Directive is unlikely to be approved until 1995 and even then it will not immediately apply to the UK. Under the Treaty of Rome either the UK Government will have to amend the 1988 Copyright Act to take into account the terms of the Directive or it does nothing when the wording of the Directive becomes UK law two years later. Readers should keep a close eye on the wording of the Directive when it finally completes its legislative process.

In this messy situation the natural thing to do is to rely on contracts. Assuming the contracts are fair, they form a basis for the relationship between the database producer and the database searcher and you should follow the ground rules in them. If you are unhappy with any of the restrictions you should contact the database producer, CD-ROM publisher or online host and negotiate; they are usually prepared to at least consider some changes to their standard contract. If you cannot agree what you can and cannot do, you are limited by fair dealing provisions. In the case of full text, you can handle it as if it were the equivalent printed material. In the case of compilations comprising facts or other non-copyright material, you may download and store a reasonable sub-set of data as long as the owner's commercial interests are not damaged. In the case of abstracts services, there is virtually nothing you can do under fair dealing. Finally, be aware that if the database is available online, some commentators believe even fair dealing does not apply. This may be a minority view but until the question is tested in the courts ...

Further Reading

PHILLIPS, Jeremy and FIRTH, Alison. *Introduction to intellectual property law*. Butterworths, 1990, is a rigorous law book which is written in a light and witty style. It has a section on electronic databases.

MARRETT, Paul. *Information law*. Gower, 1991, is written from an information professional's point of view.

OPPENHEIM, Charles. The legal and regulatory environment for electronic information, *Infonortics*, 1992, covers data protection, liability for information provision, freedom of information, database search confidentiality and other related topics as well as copyright – in more depth than in this chapter.

WALL, Ray. *Copyright in polytechnic and university libraries* and others in the same series, single copies free of charge from the Library Association. Each one of these pamphlets covers electronic copyright amongst other topics. Wall is the prime exponent of the view that online databases are both 'literary works' and 'cable programmes', and his comments on that topic should be treated with caution.

Commission of the European Communities. *Proposal for a Council Directive on the legal protection of databases.* COM(92) 24 FINAL. The Commission, 1992.
Useful articles include:

BARRETT, D. and COULTER, C. Proposed Council Directive on the legal protection of databases. *Computer Law and Practice*, 8 (2), 1992, 34-37.

GOLDING, P. The Database Directive: issues arising. *Information World Review*, March 1993, 20-21.

KUNZLICK, P. Proposed EC Council Directive on the legal protection of databases. *The Computer Law and Security Report*, 8, 1992, 116-120.

MORTON, J. Draft EC Directive on the protection of electronic databases. *Computer Law and Practice*, 8 (2), 1992, 38-45.

Appendix 1 Contact addresses for leading bibliographic software packages

Since all the packages originate in the USA the address of the software producer is given as well as the address of the main distributor in the UK. Readers in other countries will have their enquiries forwarded to the local distributor.

The suppliers have agreed to provide readers of this book with a demonstration copy of the package. Please specify the platform (Apple Mac or PC compatible) and the disk type when requesting a demonstration copy

EndNote Plus

In the USA

>Niles and Associates,
>800 Jones St.,
>Berkeley,
>CA 94710,
>USA.
>Tel: (1) 510 559 8592

For information about the *EndNote* User Group in the USA contact:

Appendix 1

> Steven K. Bang,
> 6643 Abrego Road,
> Goleta,
> CA 93117,
> USA.
> E-mail: skbang@ucsbuxa.ucsb.edu

The User Group maintains an archive and discussion list on the Internet (see Appendix 3 for details).

In the UK and Europe

> Cherwell Scientific Publishing,
> The Magdalen Centre,
> Oxford Science Park,
> Oxford OX4 4GA.
> Tel: 01865-784800

Papyrus

In the USA

> Research Software Design
> 2718 SW Kelly St.,
> Suite 181,
> Portland,
> OR 97201,
> USA.
> Tel: (1) 503 796 1368

In the UK and Europe
Universities, colleges and certain museums in the UK and Irish Republic can take advantage of the site licence agreement negotiated by the Combined Higher Educational Software Team (CHEST) with Research Software Design. For further details contact:

CHEST,
Bath University Computing Service,
Claverton Down,
Bath,
BA2 7AY.
Tel: 01225-826282

Details of the CHEST *Papyrus* discussion list on JANET are given in Appendix 3.

Other organisations in the UK can obtain *Papyrus* from:

Europa Scientific Software Corp.,
c/o Crawford Scientific,
66 Kirk Street,
Strathhaven,
ML10 6LB.
Tel: 01357-22961

Pro-Cite

In the USA

Personal Bibliographic Software Inc.,
PO Box 4250,
Ann Arbor,
MI 48106,
USA.
Tel: (1) 313 996 1580

In the UK and Europe

Personal Bibliographic Software (Europe),
Woodside,
Hinksey Hill,
Oxford OX1 5AU.
Tel: 01865-326612

For information about the UK *Pro-Cite* User Group contact:

Appendix 1

Janice Chambers,
Merck Sharp & Dohme Research Laboratories,
Terlings Park,
Eastwick Rd.,
Harlow,
Essex CM20 2QR.
Tel: 01279-440130

Reference Manager

In the USA

Research Information Systems
2355 Camino Vida Roble,
Carlsbad,
CA 92009-1572,
USA.
Tel: (1) 619 438 5526
E-Mail: risinfo@ris.risinc.com

In the UK and Europe

Research Information Systems
Building 1,
Brunel University Science Park,
Kingston Lane,
Uxbridge,
UB8 3PQ,
Tel: 01895-813544

Bilaney Consultants,
St. Julians,
Sevenoaks,
Kent TN1 1BA.
Tel: 01732-450002

Specialist formatting packages

Headform

>Head Software International
>Oxted Mill,
>Spring Lane,
>Oxted,
>Surrey,
>RH8 9PB.
>Tel: 01883-717057

RefWriter

>Tailored Information Ltd.,
>119 High Street South,
>Rushden,
>Northants,
>NN10 0RB.
>Tel: 01933-311013

Appendix 2 BIDS and bibliographic software

BIDS stands for Bath Information and Data Services and is a range of bibliographic databases mounted on computers at Bath University and accessible by British universities via the JANET network. This arrangement was negotiated by the Combined Higher Education Software Team (CHEST) and now covers the three major *Citation Indexes* and *Index to Scientific and Technical Proceedings* from ISI, *Embase* (Exerpta Medica), *Inside Information* (general current awareness database from the British Library), *Compendex*, the engineering database, and most recently, *IBSS Online* (the International Bibliography of the Social Sciences published by BLPES). Information about BIDS is available on a World Wide Web server on the Internet (the URL is: http://www.bids.ac.uk/).

Since the beginning of the BIDS service four years ago there has been growing interest in downloading and importing into personal database software. As with other database services it would be easiest and most convenient for the user if the records could be downloaded in a software-specific format such that the records would not need to be converted. But, as with the vast majority of other databases this is not the case with BIDS although who knows what may happen in the future. In the meantime, if you wish to import records into leading bibliographic software packages you will have to reformat them first. To do so you could either write a little utility yourself or adapt the reformatting module that accompanies your favourite bibsoft package (if it is adaptable).

Many people have taken the former route and have made their efforts known through various online discussion lists. These 'announcements' have now been gathered together by David Zeitlyn, chairman of the BIDS User Group, and placed in a separate file (H2AO2X) on BUBL (the Bulletin Board for Libraries). Included in the file are procedures for taking BIDS records into *Pro-Cite, Reference Manager, EndNote, ENDNote PLUS, Papyrus, BIBTEX, Idealist* and *REFER*.

Appendix 3 Internet discussion lists for bibliographic software

An online discussion lists is an E-mail based discussion forum for all those interested in a particular topic. If you have access to Janet and the Internet you can 'sign up' for hundreds of these services and begin to receive, probably, hundreds of messages. These may take the form of questions, answers, announcements, comments, complaints, etc.

In recent years the following five lists have started for users of bibliographic software packages. Where a list is on Bitnet both the Bitnet and the Internet addresses are given.

BIBSOFT@INDYCMS.BITNET or BIBSOFT@INDYCMS.IUPUI.EDU
For users of any package. This list discusses items of interest across the board. Discussions frequently centre on comparative features and performance of the leading packages.

The other four listed concentrate on particular packages:

ENDNOTE@UCSBVM.BITNET or
ENDNOTE@UCSBVM.UCSB.EDU
(Covers *EndNote* and *EndLink*)

LIBMAST@UOTTAWA.BITNET or
LIBMAST@ACADVM1.UOTTAWA.CA
(Covers the *Library Master* package)

CHEST-PAPYRUS@UK.AC.MAILBASE
(Covers the *Papyrus* package)

PRO-CITE@IUBVM.UCS.INDIANA.EDU
(Covers *Pro-Cite* and *Biblio-Links*)

RIS-LIST@RIS.RISINC.COM
(Covers Reference Manager and *Capture Module)*

Subscribing

To subscribe to any of these services you should send the following E-mail message to LISTSERV@NODE where NODE is the part of the address after the @ character:

SUBSCRIBE LIST FIRSTNAME LASTNAME

For example if John Smith wishes to subscribe to the BIBSOFT list he would type:

SUBSCRIBE BIBSOFT JOHN SMITH

For a list of lists in library-related or any other area see the appropriate section of BUBL.

Appendix 4 List of criteria for evaluation of bibliographic software

Initial screen

1. Hardware requirements (RAM, ROM)
2. Cost
3. Ability to handle bibliographic data

Nieuwenhuysen's criteria (1)

4. Input – manual, editor, word processor, non-ASCII, import downloaded records, reformatting facilities
5. Indexing – case sensitivity, stop words, basic index, inverted file, full-text
6. Information retrieval – Boolean, wild card, combine sets, proximity, display index, save searches, reuse sets, sort hits, screen display options
7. Output – select fields to display, select records from set, reformat for word processor, interface with other applications

More detailed criteria

8. Database capacity – multiple databases, numbers of records, total size of database
9. Record size – full text, numbers of fields, size of fields

10 Fields – variable length, maximum length, defaults, user defined, flexibility, multiple value e.g. authors
11 Record types – system defaults, user defined
12 Time taken to perform basic functions – searching, indexing, importing, etc.
13 Help – online, in context, user manual, hot-line support, vendor approachability
14 Ease of use – screen layout, system prompts, getting started, quitting

Additional VOGIN criteria (2, 3)

15 Thesaurus
16 Recovery from damage
17 Comprehensibility of manual
18 Reorganise database – e.g. add new field, re index existing records
19 Intervene manually during importing of downloaded records
20 Password security
21 Left hand truncation in searching
22 Duplicate checking

Additional Thornton criteria (see Chapter 7)

23 Users' reactions
24 Compatibility with existing systems

References

1 NIEUWENHUYSEN, P. Criteria for the evaluation of text storage and retrieval software. Electronic Library 6 (3) 1988, 160-166.

2 SIEVERTS, E. G. et al., *Microcomputer applications for online and local information systems: a test and comparison of 30 packages.* Leiden: VOGEN, 1987

Appendix 4

3 SIEVERTS, E. G. et al., Software for information storage and retrieval tested, evaluated and compared (in four parts). Part 1, *Electronic Library* 9 (3), 1991, 145-154; Part 2, 9 (6), 1991, 301-316; Part 3, 10 (1), 1992, 5-18; Part 4, 10 (4), 1992, 195-207.

Appendix 5 User trial questionnaire

Database Name:

Price: ☐ Within price range
☐ Perhaps affordable
☐ Out of price range

☐ Easy to use
☐ Fairly easy to use
☐ Difficult

Comments:

_____

_____

_____

Layout of screen ☐ Good
☐ Satisfactory
☐ Unsatisfactory

Appendix 5

Comments:

_____
_____
_____

Online help   ☐ Good
☐ Satisfactory
☐ Unsatisfactory
☐ Did not use

Comments:

_____
_____
_____

Manual input   ☐ Easy
☐ Satisfactory
☐ Difficult

Comments

_____
_____
_____

Single term   ☐ Easy
searching   ☐ Satisfactory
                    ☐ Difficult

Comments:

_____

_____

_____

And/Or searching   ☐ Easy
                           ☐ Satisfactory
                           ☐ Difficult

Comments:

_____

_____

_____

Multiple term   ☐ Easy
searching   ☐ Satisfactory
                    ☐ Difficult

Comments:

_____

_____

_____

Appendix 5

Quitting   ☐ Easy
☐ Satisfactory
☐ Difficult

Comments:

_____

_____

_____

Additional overall comments:

_____

_____

_____

_____

Selective bibliography

This bibliography is included as a one-stop convenient listing of recent references on bibliographic software. With few exceptions only items published since 1991 are included. The reference lists appended to the chapters will include some older material but there are some references below which do not appear in any of the reference lists.

ARONSON, A.R. *Pro-Cite. JAMA – Journal of the American Medical Association* 270 (14), 1993, 1751.

BEGG, P. *EndNote. Personal Computer World*, 15 (2), 1992, 154-156.

BEISER, K. Micro formats and software – QCLIF, *Xbase, Pro-Cite*, and *Lantastic. Computers in Libraries* 13 (4), 1993, 45.

BELLARBY, L. A comparison of two personal bibliographic software packages: *EndNote* and *Pro-Cite*. *Law Librarian* 24 (1), 1993, 22.

BIGGS, Deb Renee (Editor). *Pro-Cite in libraries: a complete guide*. Meckler, 1994.

BLUMENTHAL, E.Z. and GILAD, R. Storing a bibliographic database on your PC: a review of reference management software. *Journal of Medicine* 329 (4), 1993, 283-284.

BOLTON, W. *Papyrus. Computers and the Humanities*, 26, 1992, 162-164.

BROWN, C.C. Creating automated bibliographies using Internet – accessible online library catalogs. *Database* 17 (1), 1994, 67-71.

BUTLER, J.T. A current awareness service using microcomputer databases and electronic mail. *College and Research Libraries* 54 (2), 1993, 115-123.

COALE, K. Advances in text retrieval. *Macworld* 10 (12), 1993, 168-172.

COHEN, S.D. *EndNote Plus*: reference formatter and compiler. *Information Today* 8 (3), 1991, 35-36.

CORNELL, A.M. and PALKOVIC, M. *Pro-Cite* 2.0. RQ 32 (2), 1992, 270-271.

COX, J. Software reviews: *EndNote Plus. International Journal of Information Management* 12 (4), 1992, 327-330.

COX, J. and HANSON, T. Setting up an electronic current awareness service. *Online* 16 (4), 1992, 36-43.

DAVNALL, S. Bibliographic software for PCs. ESRC *Data Archive Bulletin (Insert: Software Bulletin No. 30)* (50), 1992, S1-S2.

DELOZIER, E.P. Bibliography nanagement with *Pro-Cite* version 2.0. *Medical Reference Services Quarterly* 12 (2), 1993, 19.

DELOZIER, E.P. Bibliography management with *Library Master* version 2.0. *Medical Reference Services Quarterly* 13 (2), 29-44.

DOHERTY, F.J. and FARQUHAR, I.K. *Pro-Cite, EndNote* and *Reference Manager. Computer Applications in the Biosciences* 7 (1), 1991, 128-132.

DOLAN, D.R. *Pro-Cite* for the IBM. *Database* 15 (5), 1992, 112.

DUDLEY, H. Personal bibliographic databases on the Macintosh: a comparison between *Pro-Cite* version 2.1 and *EndNote Plus* version 1.3. *Binary Computing in Microbiology* 5 (6), 1993, 183.

EndNote Plus: a bibliography maker for the researcher. *Library Software Review* 12 (3), 1993, 12.

FAUGHNAN, J.G. *EndNote Plus, PC-LIT* and *Reference Manager* PC. *Journal of Family Practice* 37 (3), 1993, 297.

FAUGHNAN, J.G. *Reference Manager* PC. *Journal of Family Practice* 37 (1), 1993, 92-93.

FINNIGAN, G.L. Document delivery gets personal. *Online* 16 (3), 1992, 106-108.

FRANK, O.R. Medical reference filing systems. *Australian Family Physician* 20, 1991, 57-59.

GROSCH, A.N. *Library Master*: bibliographic and textual database software. *Online Review* 14 (6), 1990, 409-414.

HANSON, T. Bibliographic databases, downloading and personal bibliographic software. *Computer Applications in the Social Sciences* 2 (1), 1991, 35-40.

HANSON, T. Bibliographic software update. In: ARMSTRONG, C.J. and HARTLEY, R.J. (eds.) *Database 2000: UKOLUG state of the art conference 1992*. Learned Information/UKOLUG, 1992, 19-29.

HANSON, T. CD-ROM, downloading and related management issues, *in*: HANSON, T. and DAY, J. (eds.) *CD-ROM in libraries*: management issues. Bowker-Saur, 1994, 193-206.

HANSON, T. Downloading and post-processing, *in*: BURTON, P.F. and MOORE, C. (eds.) *CD-ROM: a practical guide for information professionals*. London: LITC/UKOLUG, 1994, 39-43.

HANSON, T. The electronic current awareness service and the use of *Pro-Cite* at Portsmouth Polytechnic, *in*: RAITT, D.I. (ed.) *Online Information 90. 14th International Online Information Meeting, Proceedings*. Learned Information, 1990, 277-287.

HANSON, T. Getting to grips with the information explosion. *Physics World* (February), 1992, 58-59.

HANSON, T. Libraries, universities and bibliographic software. *British Journal of Academic Librarianship* 7(1), 1992, 45-54.

HANSON, T. Managing personal files. *Times Higher Educational Supplement* (15 June), 1990, Information Technology Section, VIII-IX.

HANSON, T. *The Papyrus* Bibliography system. *Library Micromation News* (31), 1991, 5-8.

HANSON, T. Personal bibliographic software and the provision of computer-based information services in academic communities. *Aslib Proceedings* 41 (9), 1989, 267-274.

HANSON, T. *Pro-Cite* Version 2: a Review. *Health Libraries Review* 10 (1), 1993, 46-49.

HANSON, T. The STN Personal File System. *Library Micromation News* (33), 1991, 33-36

HANSON, T. Using *Pro-Cite* at the University of Portsmouth, *in*: BIGGS, D. (ed.) *Pro-Cite in libraries*. Meckler, 1994.

HANSON, T. and MOORE, C. Reusing downloaded data, *in*: GUNN, A.A. and MOORE, C. (eds.) CD-ROM: *a practical guide for information professionals*. UKOLUG/LITC, 1991, 33-36.

HARTINGER, V.J. *Pro-Cite* for the Macintosh: bibliographic information manager. *Information Today* 9 (6), 1992, 17-20.

HO, B. Using *PASSPORT*, *Biblio-Links* OCLC and *Pro-Cite* to create a bibliography. OCLC MICRO 8 (5), 1992, 28.

HOKE, F. Bibliography building software eases a cruel task. *The Scientist* 7 (1), 1993, 18-19.

JONES, R.G. Personal computer software for handling references from CD-ROM and mainframe sources for scientific and medical reports. *British Medical Journal* 307 (17 July 1993), 1993, 180-184.

KELLY, J. Downloading information using bibliographic management software. *CD-ROM Professional* 7 (4), 123-6, 128.

KLEMPERER, K. *Pro-Cite* for the Macintosh. *Information Technology and Libraries* 12 (2), 1993, 291-293.

LEIRS, H., and DE BRUYN, L. New ideas for personal library maintenance software. *Nature* (366, 11 November), 1993, 183-184.

LEVY, S.R. and HINEGARDNER, P.G. Teaching *Pro-Cite*: classroom instruction and consultations. *Medical Reference Services Quarterly* 11 (1), 1992, 31-38.

LIEBERMAN, J.E. *GREF2END* – a *GEOREF* to *EndNote* Bibliography translator written in AWK. *Computers and Geosciences* 18 (9), 1992, 1271-1275.

LUNDEEN, G. Bibliographic software update. *Database* 14 (6), 1991, 57-67.

LUNDEEN, G.W. and TENOPIR, C. Text retrieval software for microcomputers and beyond: an overview and a review of four Packages. *Database* 15 (4), 1992, 51-63.

MATTHEWS, H.R. BIDSLINK: a computer program for translating references downloaded from the Bath ISI service. *Journal of Physiology* (467), 1993, 239.

MATUS, N. and BEUTLER, E.B. *Reference Update* and *Reference Manager*: personal computer programs for locating and managing references. *BioTechniques* 7 (6), 1989, 636-639.

MCINTOSH, P. Scientific current awareness in an international pharmaceutical R&D environment. *Aslib Proceedings* 45 (3), 1993, 83-87.

MEAD, T. Making the link: importing downloaded bibliographic references to *Pro-Cite* and *EndNote* on the Macintosh. *Database* 14 (1), 1991, 35-41.

MERCANDO, A.D. Managing a personal reference list by computer. *PACE-Pacing Clinical Electrophysiology* 16 (7 Pt. 1), 1993, 1423-1426.

MILLER, M.C. Reference management software: a review of *EndNote Plus, Reference Manager* and *Pro-Cite*. MD Comput. 1994, 11 (3), 161-8.

MORGAN, P. *Papyrus* Bibliography System, Version 7.0. *Binary Computing in Microbiology* 5 (3), 1993, 86.

MYERS, C.J., LESSMANN, J.J. and MUSSELMAN, R.L. A chemical literature management system using *EndNote*. *Science and Technology Libraries* 12 (2), 1992, 17.

NEAL, P.R. Personal bibliographic software programs: a comparative review. *BioScience* 43 (1), 1993, 44-51.

NELSON. F.E. Computerised personal bibliography management. *Professional Geographer*, 43, 1991, 205-211.

RABINOVITZ, R. Bibliographic software: point of reference. *PC Magazine (US Edition)* 12 (17), 1993, 269.

RAEDER, A. *Library Master* for databases and bibliographies. *Database* 14 (2), 1991, 67-72.

ROTH, D.L. *Pro-Cite* for the Macintosh version 2.0. *Journal of Chemical Information and Computer Sciences* 33 (1), 1993, 179.

SATYAMURTI, S. *EndNote Plus* – enhanced reference database and bibliography maker. *JAMA – Journal of the American Medical Association* 269 (24), 1993, 3163.

SESSIONS, R. SRS II: bibliographic software for the Macintosh. *Database* 14 (6), 1991, 54-56.

SIEVERTS, E.G. and Hofstede, M. Software for information storage and retrieval tested, evaluated and compared. Part 1: General introduction. *Electronic Library* 9 (3), 1991, 145-154.

SIEVERTS, E.G. et al. Software for information storage and retrieval tested, evaluated and compared. Part 2: Classical retrieval systems. *Electronic Library* 9 (6), 1991, 301-316.

SIEVERTS, E.G. et al. Software for information storage and retrieval tested, evaluated and compared. Part 3: End-user software. *Electronic Library* 10 (1), 1992, 5-18.

SIEVERTS, E.G. et al. Software for information storage and retrieval tested, evaluated and compared. Part 4: Indexing and full text retrieval packages. *Electronic Library* 10 (4), 1992, 195-207.

SIEVERTS, E.G. et al. Software for information storage and retrieval tested, evaluated and compared. Part 5: Personal information managers. *Electronic Library* 10 (6), 1992, 339-357.

SIEVERTS, E.G. et al. Software for information storage and retrieval tested, evaluated and compared. Part 6: Various additional programs. *Electronic Library* 11 (2), 1993, 73-91.

SIEVERTS, E.G. and HOFSTEDE, M. Software for information storage and retrieval tested, evaluated and compared. Part 7: What to choose, or the purpose of it all. *Electronic Library* 12 (1), 1994, 21-27.

SILBERGER, R. *Reference Manager* professional edition version 5.06. *Stem Cells* 11 (6), 1993, 568-570.

SILBERT, P.L. and MOORE, J.L. *Papyrus*, version 7.0 – the *Papyrus* bibliography system. *JAMA – Journal of the American Medical Association* 270 (18), 1993, 2232.

STIGLEMAN, S. *Bibliography formatting software*. Institute for Academic Technology, 1991.

STIGLEMAN, S. Bibliography formatting software: a buying guide. *Database* 15 (1), 1992, 15-27.

STIGLEMAN, S. *EndNote Plus*: Macintosh bibliography power on a PC. *Database* 15 (5), 1992, 50-55.

STIGLEMAN, S. *Papyrus*: good bibliographic value at a reasonable price. *Database* 16 (3), 1993, 82-87.

STIGLEMAN, S. *Pro-Cite* 2.0: steady evolution. *Database* 15 (6), 1992, 68-72.

STIGLEMAN, S. Bibliography formatting software: an updated buying guide for 1994. *Database* 17 (6), 1994, 53-64.

TONSING, R.E. Downloading and reformatting external records for researchers' personal databases. *Program 25* (4), 1991, 303-317.

Total information management using *Reference Update, Reference Manager* and online CD-ROM services. *FASEB Journal 7* (7), 1993, 1314.

VALAUSKAS, E. J. Indexing magazines with bibliographic software on the Macintosh. *Database* 17(3), 101-4.

WHITE, F. *EndNote* Plus – a bibliography maker for the researcher. *Library Software Review* 12 (3), 1993, 12-23.

WILLIAMSON, L. Information management solutions from Personal Bibliographic Software. *Database* 14 (3), 1991, 90-92.

WILSON, T.D. Software reviews: *Pro-Cite* version 2.0. *International Journal of Information Management* 13 (3), 1993, 235-236.

WOLFF, T.E. *Library Master* version 2.0: steady improvement for "one of the best". *Database* 16 (6), 1993, 68.

WOLFF, T.E. Personal bibliographic databases: an industrial scientist's perspective. *Database* 15 (2), 1992, 34-40.

WRIGHT, K. Bibliographic database management in an R&D environment: information specialists helping end-users. *Database* 15 (3), 1992, 35-40.

YODER, L. *Pro-Cite* – a bibliographic management program. *Nursing Research* 41 (6), 1992, 380.

ZAROUKIAN, M.H. Managing bibliographies. *Medical Software Review* 2 (2), 1993.

Notes on contributors

Eddie Carter
Eddie Carter has a degree in chemistry from Leeds University and, since 1987 been an information scientist at Thornton Research Centre near Chester. He is also database administrator for Thornton's in-house text databases running under BASIS software.

John Cox
John Cox is now Head of Information Services at the Wellcome Centre for Medical Science but was formerly Head of Information Services at the Royal Free Hospital School of Medicine, London. Until 1989 he was Engineering Information Specialist at Aston University. He is a member of the Management Committee of the UK Online User Group and is author of *Keyguide to Information Sources in Online and CD-ROM Database Searching* (London, Mansell, 1991) and a number of articles on CD-ROM, bibliographic software and electronic current awareness services.

Sarah Davnall
Sarah Davnall joined Manchester University's Computing Centre as a programmer in 1976 following several years in industry. In 1985 she moved into general user support, subsequently specialising in the support of database

management software. Following the University's adoption of *Papyrus* as its bibliographic software in 1991, support for this package became her primary function until she was recently transferred to other work.

Terry Hanson
As this book went to press Terry Hanson took up a post as Head of Research and Information Services at the University of Connecticut. He was formerly Sub-Librarian for Electronic Information Services at the University of Portsmouth where he was also responsible for social sciences and official publications. He has published widely on bibliographic software and its applications, CD-ROM and information networking, European Community information and on social science information and was founder and first Chairman of the UK Pro-Cite User Group.

Jane Milligan
Jane Milligan is Technical Services Librarian at the Library of the Imperial Cancer Research Fund, London where she has been since 1980. Prior to this she worked at Sheffield University Library in a variety of capacities. At the ICRF she has been involved in providing current awareness services using ISI Science Citation Index source tapes and co-ordinating the use of *EndNote*.

Charles Oppenheim
Charles Oppenheim is Professor and Head of the Department of Information Science, University of Strathclyde, Glasgow. Prior to taking up this appointment he was Business Development Manager with Reuters Ltd. He is a Fellow of the Institute of Information Scientists and a former Vice Chairman of its Council and is a former Chairman of the UK Online User Group. He is Vice President of Aslib and a Fellow of the Library Association. He is one of four UK representatives on the EC Commission's Legal Advisory Board. He has written and spoken extensively on patents, copyright, data protection, information policy, online information and CD-ROM, etc.

David Slee
David Slee is currently a Senior Lecturer in law at the Centre for Legal Studies, University of Hertfordshire and visiting lecturer and consultant to a number of bodies in both the public and private sector. His main interests are in the areas of intellectual property and product liability with particular reference to computers and computerised information and control systems.